Pilgrims in Mission

Celebrating 150 years of the English Presbyterian Mission

ISBN 0 9533153 0 4

Published in 1998
by George Hood
1 Royal Oak Gardens, Alnwick, Northumberland NE66 2DA

in association with the

United Reformed Church
86 Tavistock Place
London WC1H 9RT

Copyright

With one exception, the copyright for the Memories, pp 46-151 belongs in each case to the individual contributors, named in the text. The copyright for pp 68-71 belongs to the *International Bulletin of Missionary Research* and is reproduced with permission. The Order of Service on pp 152-169 was written for the 1997 Assembly of the United Reformed Church and is used with permission. Apart from these, the copyright rests with the compiler, part author and publisher, George Hood.

All rights reserved. No part of this publication may be reproduced, stored in a retrieval system, or transmitted in any form, electronic, mechanical, photocopying, recording, or other means without the prior permission in writing of the publisher.

Printed by Aln Printers, Alnwick

CONTENTS

Forewords: David Jenkins, Moderator, United Reformed Church, 1997-1998   2
Arthur Macarthur, General Secretary, Presbyterian Church of England, 1960-1972   3

Acknowledgements   6

Introduction   7

From 1847 to 1997   9

The English Presbyterian Mission Withdrawal from China   25

Memories   South Fujian and East Guangdong (Swatow/Hakka):   46
Downward, Latto, Milne, Tully, Strange, Waddell

Taiwan: 66
Anderson, Beeby, Moody, Landsborough, Crofts, Whitehorn, Storey, Carruthers, Barclay, Shepherd, Riddoch, Brown

Singapore and Malaysia: 104
Sirkett, Atherton, Henderson, Hood, Swanston, Dukes, Marsden

East Pakistan/ Bangladesh: 127
Macleod, Dawson, Patrick, Hope, Saunders, Irving, Degenhardt, Morgan

The Service of Thanksgiving, 9 July, 1997   152

List of English Presbyterian missionaries   170

Maps   44, 45, 65, 103, 126

Photographs   i to xvi

FOREWORD

All cultures are immensely enriched by stories which are passed on from one generation to another. Christianity began its life through a living oral tradition which was vital to its survival. The New Testament grew out of that vibrant tradition, but that wasn't the end of story-telling and the sharing of "good news of great joy for all people."

The stories of the people of faith have always nourished and encouraged the church. So this book is now generously offered to the Church. Its roots go back to the 1997 Assembly of the United Reformed Church which was held at the Guildhall, Portsmouth. At this Assembly it was decided to mark the 150th Anniversary of the English Presbyterian Mission in a significant way. As well as producing an attractive display commemorating people and events, there also took place an evening of thanksgiving and celebration. Missionaries who had served in the five 'fields' of mission were given the opportunity to record some of their experiences. Then representatives from the Christian churches now witnessing in those places also described how the legacy of the missionaries was being built upon at the present time.

Those of us who experienced this evening event were deeply moved by the stories of faith and courage which we heard. We were enabled to thank God for the commitment of past and present Christians and to rededicate our own lives to the ongoing mission of Christ in all places. What a resonance for encouragement and new life are testimonies like this. They speak of God's activity, God's outreach, God's work in every generation.

This book now digs even deeper into this rich resource and makes it available to a wider audience. We are grateful to George Hood and all who have enabled this book to be printed. May it bring delight to many readers and glory to the God whose mission we share.

David Jenkins
Moderator, United Reformed Church, 1997-1998

FOREWORD

It is with admiration and gratitude that I salute this further work of my old Sunday School friend and respond to his request that I should add this foreword. Quite apart from his direct missionary service, George has done great work since retirement in connection with the Friends of the Church in China and in proper recall of the years of missionary endeavour sustained by the English Presbyterians before 1972. Beth, his wife, has been his companion and support in everything, carrying on the heritage of her father Douglas James, who was taken from his own great labours by the appalling loss we suffered when the rocket destroyed Church House in February 1945. Like other missionary wives she was never on the payroll and her name is on no official list but her service is written in the life of the Chinese and Malaysian Churches.

Like others brought up in the Presbyterian Church of England, overseas mission was in my blood stream from before birth. My aunt served as an E.P. missionary for twenty years in South Fujian and was home on furlough the year before I was born. Such furloughs were then few and far between and were largely spent 'on deputation'. Both single and married missionaries accepted the pain of long periods of separation from their families as part of their commitment. For those blest with children there was the further agonising dilemma of choosing between separation from partner or children. for years at a time.

In our Sunday School childhood, George and I shared in a Missionary Alphabet, he was Amoy and I was Wukingfu. As a senior schoolboy I was on the Formosa stall at a missionary exhibition in the Assembly Rooms in Newcastle in the company of Sabine Mackintosh, one of the three WMA missionaries who died in a Japanese prison camp. At Westminster College we had two missionaries home to train for ordination having already served as educationists. Tim Manson's deep convictions had much to do with Alan Macleod's offer for service in India. (Ten years later, during the Mission Centenary Assembly in Newcastle, in 1947, I recall Alan successfully challenging the whole denomination to support its Rajshahi Mission more effectively or else.....) None of us was quite the same after we had encountered the flaming sacrificial zeal of Reg Mobbs. Offered sixpence for overseas mission if he walked round the tennis court barefoot in the snow, his socks were off at once. Needless to say we increased the reward but he would have settled for the 'tanner'. Ian Latto, still playing tennis, Robert Richards and Lesslie Newbigin were already committed to their future work. Missionaries visited and stayed in the College, and the FM Secretary came regularly, 'head-hunting' and challenging us with needs and opportunities of service overseas. In those days overseas fellow-students were more likely to be from the USA, Commonwealth or European countries, but before long there was to be an outstanding succession of men and women from Asia and Africa who personalised the world church in our everyday life.

And then there was the College Missionary Society, linking up the students, the congregations and the work of mission. It was part of our education, our training for the ministry. Every year, after full debate - a lesson in itself - we adopted some particular cause for the 'Plea'. This was usually an overseas project or need. We swotted up the subject and then went out to churches all over the country as its advocates. Fees earned were handed over along with the special offerings received. So although, like many others, I never saw any of our work overseas at first hand I felt it to be as integral a part of the enterprise of the Church as the vigorous church extension policy we pursued at home.

Another great influence both personally and in the life of the Church, at home and overseas was the Fellowship of Youth. It was a seed-bed for the ministry and for Christian service of every kind. Many of those who have shared their 'Memories' will be recognised as having been part of that Fellowship. As missionaries on furlough they may also recall attending Youth Conferences, and, after an absence of five years, finding or failing to find themselves on the changing wave-lengths of youth.

As a minister in pastoral charge I also experienced the value and encouragement of missionary service by members from the congregations I served. In New Barnet the 'extended family' of Maclagans, Dales and Richards provided a dimension to the congregation and contribution to the English Presbyterian Mission which must be almost unique. In North Shields I was very aware of the Barclay contribution, past and future and also had the joy of seeing one of my own young people, Jim Swanston, being ordained to the missionary eldership for service in Malaysia. I had helped with his wedding in the far north of Scotland and seeing them off with Catherine already expecting their first child, gave me a new and personal appreciation of the cost of being a missionary.

Both in my home and in all the churches I served the Women's Missionary Association (WMA) which for long employed and paid its own missionaries, was both effective in recruitment and constant in its communication to the local congregations of missionary experience overseas. Its officers, paid or voluntary, were honoured in the Church and significant in its outlook and enterprise. With nearly a century of service, their acceptance of the terms of union in 1972 which 'abolished' the Association was evidence of a loyalty that had always been part of a larger whole.

As General Secretary of the denomination from 1960 I had this inbred understanding and enthusiasm for the work and found co-operation with Reg Fenn and later Boris Anderson, the full time secretaries concerned with the overseas side, enriching and a healthy reminder that Mission is the name of the game. As 1972 drew near Boris was prophetic in his insistence that a new age had dawned, an age of interdependence and partnership. He was rightly afraid that concern for the shaping of the new Church in England might miss that dawn. Traditionally we had made much of our relationships with sister churches in Europe and America but now through past missionary endeavour we were part of a wider family. The creation of a World Church and Mission Department gave Mission a central place in the life of the Church and also expressed the church to church relationships which must now exist. And it was this insight and vision which he with others carried through in creating the new Council for World Mission in 1975.

The stories of daily excitement, frequent heroism and humble service that follow are part of our heritage of faith. That heritage now mingles with the wider, richer and often more heroic experience of those in our partner churches whose courage and hope seem often to rebuke our complacency and our anxiety. The events which George describes, leading to the enforced withdrawal of missionaries from China is also a major part of that heritage. For the Church in China it was a necessary step in its pilgrimage but for those involved a time of sadness, painful separations and bewilderment - a reminder of the high cost of mission to those who have to shape it in the turbulence of history. It is indeed a privilege to commend this book with its human lights as well as its vital questions.

Yours in gratitude

Arthur Macarthur

ACKNOWLEDGEMENTS

In my introduction I refer to many of those who helped to produce this book. From some who wrote their memories I also received photographs, namely Walter Carruthers, with the extra bonus of his photography expertise, Elizabeth Brown, Margaret Macleod, Joyce Saunders, David Morgan and Jean Degenhardt. Some photographs originally appeared in English Presbyterian publications and permission to reproduce them is gratefully acknowledged. The three pictorial maps were drawn by John Whitehorn in 1962, and although outdated by church growth and political changes are very representative of the period and worthy of reprinting.

From the United Reformed Church, the Barbour Trust, and the Carmichael-Montgomery Trust I have also received generous grants which have enabled the book to be published. I also appreciate the encouragement and practical help which Philip Woods and Naomi Young have provided throughout the past year of EP Mission celebration. Their patience has matched my persistence. And most recently Carol Rogers, Secretary for Communications has given good advice and told me as much as I needed to know about the mysteries of publishing.

After fifty-five years of marriage, Beth has learned to cope with all my changes of mood, but the "gleams of joy and clouds of doubt" which have surrounded the production of this book have been more than usual. Sufficient to say that she was even more determined than I was to see the task completed. So for that, as for so much more, I am deeply grateful.

George Hood

INTRODUCTION

Publishing a book of this kind requires explanation. In his foreword the Moderator has described the occasion which gave it birth, a service of celebration and thanksgiving for the work of the English Presbyterian Mission since its beginning in 1847. For all who attended, and especially for the former English Presbyterian missionaries it was a happy occasion to renew contact both with each other and the representatives of the churches overseas in which they had served. But it was not a nostalgia trip, and neither is this book. The inspiration and challenge which so many people found in the Thanksgiving Service was evidence of how much we can be encouraged in mission today by sharing our memories of the past.

When I heard it was planned to make the content of the Thanksgiving Service, including the texts of the brief talks given, more widely available in the denomination and beyond, I felt that this was an opportunity not to be missed. As part of the celebration an exhibition had been prepared which displayed the work of the English Presbyterian Mission (EPM) in its five areas of work, South Fujian (Amoy), East Guangdong (Lingdong, i.e. Swatow/Hakka), Taiwan (Formosa), Singapore/Malaysia, Bangladesh (Rajshahi), and focussed on three periods, the pioneer, the 1947 centenary, and the present. A small booklet had been written *1847 and All That* which served as both guide to what was displayed and an outline of the whole 150 years. Edward Band's centenary history, *Working His Purpose Out,* is now out of print, but for this celebration R.E.Fenn's book, *Working God's Purpose Out, 1947-1972,* was published and on sale. It continues the official history of the EPM up to the formation of the United Reformed Church in 1972.

1847 and All That, re-named *From 1847 to 1997,* and slightly enlarged, is included as a first chapter in the present book to provide some necessary historical background for both the Thanksgiving Service and the Memories which form its larger part. It is in no way even the merest outline history of the churches among whom EP missionaries worked. Churches must write their own history and assessment of the part missionaries played in them. But mission undertaken in the name of a church, whether at home or abroad, is part of that church's history, and needs to be known, understood and evaluated as well as we can. What is special to this book is that the last period of EP mission history is largely presented through the eyes and experience of the missionaries, adding flesh to the bare bones. The second chapter on the withdrawal of the EP missionaries from China is a fuller account than has previously been written of that most determinative event in our mission history, and begins with my reasons for writing it. It is followed by the four sections of Memories. In the first of these I have included extracts from letters of that time and from one personal memoir. The second section includes one contribution originally written for another publication, but all the others were written for this book. I am most grateful to all whom I invited, persuaded, bullied, cajoled or beguiled into writing, and amazed that in the end none refused. I am equally grateful for the freedom they allowed me to edit and attempt to keep them - not very successfully - within the limits I had set. I used some criteria, length of service and balance between areas and type of work, to decide whom to invite, and for those not invited I hope that relief will exceed regret. May I also express my thanks to the Moderator, David Jenkins, who had such a large part in designing the Thanksgiving Service, and to Arthur Macarthur for their encouragement and Forewords. At the end of the book I have included a full and I hope accurate list of missionaries, their years and area(s) of service, and type of work. The Christian names of missionary wives have been included which I hope is a more appropriate recognition of their existence and contribution than the previous asterisk!

To return to the Memories. Not all turned out as I had expected but there is sufficient variety to represent both the light and shade of missionary experience as well as the wide spectrum of character and service. By sharing their memories the writers present a picture of what the last generation of those who went out as EP missionaries were doing, and that is of historical interest. They may also help to demolish some missionary stereotypes which still haunt us. But more important than that. I hope they will help to bring home the rich experience of working alongside, at every level, our Christian brothers and sisters of different cultures, and perhaps make some of them more real to us. A suitable title still eludes me - and others from whom I have sought suggestions - but I think *Pilgrims in Mission* comes nearest, embracing churches celebrating anniversaries, partnership around the world, and our individual discipleship.

The cover of the book represents *Pilgrims in Mission*. On the back is one of the illustrations, dated 1860, of *Pilgrim* leaving home, from William Burns' translation into Chinese of Bunyan's *Pilgrim's Progress*. The background to the front cover shows modern missionary travel in Bangladesh, getting out of the Land Rover to "make the rough places plain".

FROM 1847 TO 1997

When the Presbyterian Church was reconstituted in England in 1843, one of its first decisions was to appoint a committee for Foreign Missions. In this it followed the pattern of both the Church of Scotland and the Free Church of Scotland, that mission should be the responsibility of the whole church and not just of a voluntary society. This was a high ideal. Although in practice there were many, perhaps even a majority of members, who were not actively concerned, 'foreign' or as it was later called 'overseas' mission had its place at the centre of the church's life and structure. The missionaries appreciated the fact that they were sent out in the name of the whole church, and valued their right to be members of the General Assembly. The fact that so many of them either during or after their missionary service became moderators of the General Assembly or held other high office testifies to this close link.

The same year, 1843, also saw the end of the first Opium War against China, and the Treaty of Nanking which ceded Hong Kong and gave a limited opening to foreign trade and foreign missionaries. While other mission bodies were rejoicing in this long awaited opportunity, the Free Church of Scotland, in spite of its enthusiasm for a China mission was in no position to undertake such a task. It had already taken over most of the foreign mission work of the pre-Disruption Church of Scotland, and that burden on top of the financial pressure at home to build churches and support a ministry, meant it was unable to take up this new opportunity of working in China. In these circumstances it was very natural that the newly formed Presbyterian Church in England, with its close links with the Free Church of Scotland, should undertake such work. The years which followed, especially the first fifty, showed how great a support was provided from that source. Almost all the missionaries sent out during that period came from Scotland. In addition, the Scottish Auxiliary which functioned rather like a missionary society within the Free Church, provided the financial support of a large number of them.

The first missionary

Although the Foreign Missions Committee existed from 1843, it was not until 1847 that the first missionary was appointed. William Burns from Kilsyth had already established a reputation as an evangelist in Scotland, Canada, Ireland and England, before his appointment by the

Synod, meeting in Sunderland, to work in China. It followed an approach made to him by a former fellow-student in Aberdeen, James Hamilton, minister of Regent Square Presbyterian Church, London, and convener of the FMC, and G F Barbour, a devout business man with strong links in both the Free Church of Scotland and the Presbyterian Church in England. G F Barbour was the first in a family which continued to support the EP Mission generously throughout its history.

Burns began work in Hong Kong, learning Cantonese and teaching, closely associated with the predominantly Scots group of London Missionary Society missionaries living there. He was primarily an evangelist, believing like Paul that he was called to preach rather than to baptise. Already convinced of the value of medical work to open a way for the gospel, he persuaded the FMC to employ Dr James Young, who was living in Hong Kong to work with him. Discouraged by their reception in Canton, Burns agreed with the Committee to make Amoy, another Treaty Port, their base. It meant learning another Chinese dialect, but the area was considered less antagonistic to foreigners. They arrived there in 1850.

The first 'field', Amoy/South Fujian

When Burns began his itinerant preaching in the Amoy area, missionaries of the London Missionary Society and the Dutch Reformed Church in America were already there. From the beginning there was close co-operation among the three missions and this set a pattern for the future, both locally and nationally. A second ordained EP missionary, James Johnston, who also had educational qualifications, joined him in 1853. Johnston gave up the idea of promoting an English medium education on the Indian pattern, but believed the Mission should promote Chinese medium schools, primarily for the children of church members and with a view to training a Chinese ministry. For nearly seven years Burns saw little open response to his preaching, but in 1854 the first fruits were reaped at the market town of Peh-chui-a, fifteen miles from Amoy. The remarkable development of the congregation there and the responsibility it took for evangelistic outreach in neighbouring villages became a model of church growth.

Young and Johnson were both invalided home after a short period but the principles of intensive evangelistic preaching, medical work to remove prejudice and open a way for the gospel, and educational work to build up the life of the church were already established. On his first leave

Burns recruited Carstairs Douglas, the man whose influence on the Amoy field has been most profound. To his ministry Douglas brought the qualities of a highly disciplined life and a great intellectual stamina to which the famous Hokkien (South Fujian) Dictionary he compiled is the most fitting testimony. Through the use of a romanised script the Bible and other Christian literature became the possession of the ordinary church member and this example was followed in each of the China fields. In 1877, only a few months before his death, Douglas was chosen in Shanghai to be one of the two chairmen of the first conference of Protestant missionaries in China.

The Swatow and Hakka 'fields'

During his second term Burns continued his itinerant preaching. He joined up with Hudson Taylor in the Shanghai hinterland, and the two of them then shared a simultaneous sense of being called to the area of Swatow, East Guangdong. Although it was not yet one of the Treaty Ports, they succeeded in obtaining accommodation through Burns' contacts with Cantonese traders. Still firmly convinced of the value of medical work, after Taylor's departure, and at his own expense, Burns employed a devout Christian doctor, De la Porte, to run a clinic and thereby break down prejudice and provide opportunities for friendly contacts.

Although Burns spent some time at Swatow and visited it again on other occasions, George Smith, from Aberdeen was the first missionary to reside there permanently - his first term lasted fourteen years, from 1858 to 1872. He inherited some fruits of work previously done in that area, but abandoned in despair, by the Basel Society missionary, Rudolph Lechler. In the next five years Smith was joined by another ministerial missionary, Hur Mackenzie from Inverness, and a doctor, William Gauld from Aberdeen, who founded the Swatow Mission Hospital. Ten years later, the Foreign Missions Committee, in response to urgent appeals from the Swatow missionaries, especially those of Duffus and Gibson, approved the extension of the mission work to the inland Hakka-speaking area. G F Barbour personally undertook to provide two salaries and MacIver, in 1879, and Dr Riddel, the great mapmaker, in 1881, became the first missionaries to the Hakkas.

To Swatow, in 1878, the first single woman missionary, Catherine Ricketts, was also appointed. Up to this stage, the missionary wives had played a vital role in work among women and girls, which in Swatow included the founding of the first girls' school. Although Miss Ricketts herself was financially independent, her appointment and the prospect of others to follow hastened the formation of the Women's Missionary Association in the same year. Throughout the rest of the Mission's history the WMA fulfilled many of the functions of a well-run missionary society within the overall framework of the Foreign Missions Committee, and provided the financial support of over 150 missionaries, working in every part of the Mission's life. By this time the Students' Missionary Society of the Presbyterian Church's Theological College at Queen's Square, London, later to become the Westminster College Missionary Society, was already in existence. It ensured that each trainee for the ministry was well informed of the Church's overseas work.

Taiwan, Formosa, 'the children's field'

The first steps to establish work in Taiwan (Formosa) were taken from Amoy. Most of the Chinese who had settled there in the past centuries spoke the same form of Chinese as that of South Fujian. They had pushed the original peoples into the mountains and occupied the more fertile plains. In 1865, Carstairs Douglas from Amoy accompanied a young doctor, James Maxwell, to the island to survey the possibilities. Following their recommendations, the Foreign Missions Committee approved the beginning of the mission in the southern half of the island. Very soon after, Canadian Presbyterians began work in the north. At an early stage Taiwan was designated the children's field and generations of children in the church became familiar with what Portugese sailors called the 'Isla Formosa'. The island had been the last refuge of supporters of the Ming dynasty and their Manchu conquerors had only exercised a loose control for many years. In 1885 it was given provincial status, but ten years later, by the Treaty of Shimonoseki, and in the face of much local resistance, ceded to Japan. The three major fields of English Presbyterian mission work, South Fujian (Amoy), Swatow/Hakka, and Taiwan (Formosa) were thus all opened up within fifteen years of William Burns' arrival in Amoy. In each case a broadly similar pattern of intensive itinerant preaching and church planting, medical and educational work was followed.

A fourth China related 'field ', Singapore and Malaysia

The first missionary appointed was John Bethune Cook in 1881. But Cook inherited a situation prepared by others. For many years both the missionaries in South Fujian and East Guangdong (Swatow/Hakka) and the largely expatriate Presbyterian congregation of Orchard Road, Singapore, had urged the Foreign Missions Committee to send missionaries to work there. The former were concerned for pastoral work among a number of Chinese converts from those areas who had made their way to Singapore and Malaya, and the latter were challenged by the missionary task on their doorstep. Cook also fell heir to the work done by one of the earlier group of London Missionary Society missionaries, Benjamin Keasberry, who had remained there when his colleagues departed to enter the 'open door' of China. For over 40 years Cook combined all the missionary roles, pioneer, preacher, pastor, propagandist and administrator. A presbytery was formed in 1901, but the church was very dependent on China both for its members and even more for its ministry. Financially, however, it made little demand on the Mission. For long periods Cook was on his own, and at the best of times had only one or two Chinese-speaking missionary colleagues. Good opportunities in the early days for educational work had to be abandoned for lack of staff. When he retired in 1925 the missionary presence was limited to the Malay-speaking William Murray who looked after Keasberry's former Malay Chapel and one Swatow-speaking WMA missionary, Margaret Dryburgh.

The China context

Before we look at the remaining field of English Presbyterian work it might be helpful to have in mind the historical circumstances in which so much of its work was done.

Throughout the period of the Mission's work in China there were few years of political peace or social harmony. Burns' arrival in Amoy in 1850 was the year in which the Taiping Rebellion began. That was the beginning of twelve years in which at least ten million died, a period of death and destruction from which the Manchu dynasty never fully recovered. The steady encroachment on China's sovereign power by the rapacity of Western and later Japanese imperialism fuelled both anti-dynasty and anti-foreign feeling. The Manchus were overthrown in 1911, but not before the anti-foreign feeling which had previously expressed itself in sporadic attacks on foreign lives and property was seen at its most violent in the Boxer Rising of 1900. During the following century a new Chinese nationalism developed, owing something to increased contact with western ideas but much more to the feelings of outrage at the way in which China's weaknesses had been exploited. 'Unequal Treaties' had been imposed following each of her defeats. These opened the country to foreign trade and technology but only on the terms imposed by foreign powers and in their economic interests. They also excluded foreigners from Chinese jurisdiction, and, most insidious from a Mission point of view, tempted Chinese to claim foreign protection.

China's feeling of betrayal at the Treaty of Versailles in 1919 combined with the intellectual revolution of that period and the growth of industrial labour forged an unprecedented alliance between teachers, students and workers. Nationalist feeling ran deep in both the Kuomintang and the Chinese Communist Party. Up to the 1920s Britain, by reason of past history and its major financial involvement was still the main target of that feeling, succeeded in that role by Japan and then the USA. Although the concern to keep China as an ally brought the abrogation of extraterritorial rights in 1943, anti-foreign feeling could still be stirred up when situations such as the Korean War required it.

English Presbyterian missionaries, like all others, were caught up in the dilemma of being both beneficiaries of foreign power and also its critics. However much they attacked the opium trade, sought its abolition, and cared for its causalities, in Chinese eyes they could not escape being identified with their fellow-countrymen who were involved in it or the gunboats which protected them. They were also not blind to how easily they might be manipulated to use their privileges as foreigners to protect those who *prima facie* were victims of injustice, especially as the result of Christian profession. Those missionaries who reached China after the second world war were free of the privileges which had proved such a burden on their predecessors.

Special features of each 'field'

Of the three China fields, Amoy (South Fujian) and Swatow/Hakka (Lingdong or East Guangdong) had most in common. Both suffered from local rioting, and the passage back and forth with accompanying depredations of warlord armies. In its early years Amoy had more direct experience of the Taiping Rebellion, but Lingdong was more deeply affected by political events in the 1920s, which led to the removal from Mission control of the highly-regarded Anglo-Chinese School. Both Amoy and Swatow were occupied by Japanese forces for six to seven years but their occupation extended more widely in the Swatow area. Both were among the first synods in the Church of Christ in China, in joining, and in their progress towards the target of self-support, self-government and self-propagation. Whereas the South Fujian Synod had grown out of the early close co-operation of three mission boards sharing a similar Reformed tradition and working in one Chinese dialect, the Lingdong Synod was wholly English Presbyterian in background and its two presbyteries were divided along dialect lines, Swatow (more correctly Chao-chow or Tie-chiu) and Hakka. Side by side with it was an equally strong Baptist Association of churches, the product of the American Baptist Mission.

The widespread use of a romanised script in the Church originated in Amoy, and Douglas' dictionary provided its standard. A comparable romanised for both the Chao-chow and Hakka dialects was promoted with equal enthusiasm by the missionaries in these areas but there it largely fell victim to the anti-foreign feeling of the 1920s, It lasted longer in Amoy and longer still among the Amoy-speaking Diaspora in south-east Asia. The mission-founded middle schools of the South Fujian field have also provided the nucleus of Christian congregations in that same area, notably the Philippines, Singapore, Malaysia and Indonesia.

As already noted medical work was considered an essential arm of mission in each area. The oldest Mission Hospital, that of Swatow, founded in 1863, was specially remarkable for the large number of congregations throughout the area who traced their beginnings to its grateful patients. Both there and elsewhere the doctors trained in the Mission Hospitals provided many of the lay leaders and major financial supporters of their local congregations. In the Swatow field another major financial support developed through the drawn-thread embroidery which also had a link with the hospital. There was a strong Chao-chow embroidery tradition but it was Mrs Lyall, the wife of the hospital superintendent, who first taught a patient the drawn thread skill which she herself had learned in Switzerland. From that small beginning developed both a cottage and factory industry which supplemented rural incomes and brought wealth to many church families.

The Swatow/Hakka field, in the course of its history, provided the home Church with five of its Assembly moderators. Among them, J.Campbell Gibson was the most distinguished, both for his work in China to achieve a united Chinese Church and for the part he played in the 1910 Edinburgh Conference.

In 1895 China's humiliating defeat by Japan and cession of Taiwan created a new environment for the Mission there. It brought greater stability but tighter control by the new imperial power. Japan's policy of not allowing other missionary bodies to enter apart from those already established, English Presbyterians in the south and Canadian in the north, prevented the multiplying of sometimes competing mission bodies which occurred elsewhere. Because the imperial power in this case was Japan the Christian missionary may have been spared some of the identification with imperialism which was incurred in other parts of the world. It removed one barrier of identification with the people to whom he or she had been sent. But the growth of Japanese nationalism and the issue of state Shintoism created special tensions for Church and Mission.

The pioneer missionary in Taiwan was Dr Maxwell and medical work there as in other fields has always played an important role with which two generations of both Maxwells and Landboroughs are closely associated. But theological education was also a high priority and in Taiwan is always linked with the EP Mission's longest serving missionary, Thomas Barclay, who served there for over sixty years, from 1874 to 1935. He made the Tainan Theological College, founded in 1880, his life work and 240 ministers and preachers were trained under his principalship. But equally influential was his belief in the benefits of the romanised script. In Taiwan there was less prejudice against its use which has continued to the present time.

The growing power of Japan and its imperialist designs, threatening Western interests, caused its relations with Britain to deteriorate. Anti-British feelings increased in the 1930s, and the point was reached when the missionaries felt their continued presence was causing serious difficulties for the Taiwanese Church. With sadness but in faith, at the end of 1940, the remaining missionaries, Edward Band and his four WMA colleagues, Misses Mackintosh, Cullen, Elliott and Livingston closed down the EP Mission of South Formosa. Previous to this there had been a steady process of devolvement from Mission to Church and it was a Church for which self-support was not an impossible ideal. A year later Britain declared war on Japan and there was no contact with the Church in Taiwan for over three and a half years. After the Japanese surrender and the occupation of the island by KMT forces the Church invited the Mission to return to help in its rehabilitation and that of its institutions. Amid some sombre news was the thrilling story of the underground Christian movement among the mountain tribes, previously largely untouched, and of thousands asking to be prepared for baptism.

The Japanese victories over British forces in Malaya and the fall of Singapore brought a much more dramatic end of the EP Mission there. The small number of missionaries were interned and the Church was cut off from any Mission support. Fortunately its past dependence had been comparatively small but this experience increased its determination to be self-supporting. Under Japanese occupation the Chinese, and not least the Christians among them, were all under suspicion for the help they had given to the fight against Japan in China. According to Robert Richards' report, quoted by Band, 'there was hardly a family without some relative who had disappeared and of whom there had been no news at all'. Some church buildings were burnt down, others occupied as enemy property, and others lost furniture. But the Church survived, and its Chinese leadership had proved themselves.

Reg Fenn's recently published book, *Working God's Purpose Out 1947-1972,* provides the fullest account available for that period and the background for most of the 'Memories' to be found in this book. What follows is the simplest of outlines to link the first hundred years, covered by Band's Centenary history with the last twenty-five, from 1972 to 1997.

1947-1972

In Taiwan this was an outstanding period of development in the history of the Presbyterian Church, of which the 'Memories' will provide ample evidence Blest with fine Taiwanese leadership, the Church not only recovered from its wartime traumas but went on to the 'Greater things shall you do.....' which was one of its finest leaders, Shoki Coe's favourite texts. Under his leadership and by his foresight Tainan Theological College achieved high standards of theological training and also provided other forms of training which proved invaluable for the life of the Church. The Church also seized the unexpected opportunities and special needs of the work among the tribal people and acted vigorously to meet them. Ten years before its centenary, it launched a Doubling the Church Movement which in 1965 achieved its targets both of members and congregations. The number of churches increased from 410 to 863 and the membership from 86,064 to 177,420. Of these, 398 churches and a Christian community of 75,000 were among the tribal people. This Movement sealed the unity between the north and south synods in one General Assembly which had been achieved in 1955. After its centenary it embarked on a programme of greater involvement in an increasingly industrialised society, new responsibility towards the mountain people and rural churches, and also began to send missionaries overseas, in part, but not exclusively to work among Taiwanese communities. The government policy of providing nine years free education created some difficulties for the Church's Middle schools, but at every other level, in kindergartens, through commercial, agricultural, and technical training schools, in work among students and Tunghai Christian University the Church was actively involved, as it was also in medical work

During these twenty-five years there was growing tension between church and government, often focussed on the use of the Taiwanese language and the printing and use of the Taiwanese romanised bible. This version of the bible had proved so valuable in nourishing the life of the church that prohibition of its printing was strongly resisted and regarded as an infringement of religious liberty. Out of this and the church's increasing involvement in social issues developed a wider concern for human rights, and the right of the Taiwanese people to have a say in their future, culminating in the 'Statement on the National Fate' issued in January, 1972.

Throughout this period about twenty EP missionaries, including eight of those transferred from South Fujian, were working in the church and its related institutions. But these years also brought a major change, in that English and Canadian Presbyterian Missions ceased to be the only providers of personnel and financial support.. At first the Presbyterian Church in Taiwan viewed with alarm the sudden, great influx of mission bodies, most of them American, following the withdrawal from the mainland. Being mainly Mandarin-speaking their missionaries first concentrated their efforts on the Chinese from the mainland now living in Taiwan. Political attitudes and relationships also came into the situation and increased the sense of Taiwanese identity in the Presbyterian Church. However, in the course of time. through the willingness of some mission bodies to co-operate in varying degrees, and wise leadership in the Assembly, the Church was able to benefit greatly from this widening partnership in mission.

For the church in Singapore and Malaysia 1947 to 1972 were also years of dramatic change which mirrored the political, social and economic changes of the same period. A church which had sent a delegation to the last Assembly of the Church of Christ in China, meeting in Soochow in 1948, with a view to becoming a Nanyang Synod of that body, and which would continue to call itself for many years to come 'The Singapore Malaya Synod of the Chinese Christian Church' eventually became two churches of two separate countries, the Presbyterian Church in Singapore and the Presbyterian Church in Malaysia. The triumph of communism in China and the 'Emergency' in Malaysia and Singapore ended the former easy communication, already affected by the Japanese wartime occupation, and the traditional dependence upon China for ministers and members. Theological education became a high priority and by the end of the period most of the church's ministers and preachers were 'home-grown' products of either the ecumenical Trinity Theological College or the more conservative Singapore Bible College. In the early years the opportunities presented by the New Villages in Johore were high on the agenda, but by the middle of the 1950s the Synod had recognised the growing need for English language services and accepted in principle the idea of an English medium Presbytery in the future. The end of colonial rule greatly reduced the number of British expatriates in government, industry and commerce, which affected the four largely expatriate congregations in Singapore, Kuala Lumpur, Penang and Ipoh, still part of the Presbyterian Church of England. The Synod launched its first Five Year Movement for doubling the church in 1961, partly inspired by the example of Taiwan, and took the first steps towards starting new congregations outside its traditional areas of work in Johore and the north-east.

This period saw a boom in church building as many church members no longer looked back to China, expecting to end their days in their homeland, but saw their future and that of their children in Singapore and Malaysia. This increased the demand for English-medium education. At the same time greater government involvement and demand for higher standards brought closure to some Chinese primary schools attached to congregations, while others flourished and kindergartens helped to fill a gap.

From 1947 to 1972 the Church grew steadily in numbers but more significantly its roots went deeper. It never allowed itself to be overwhelmed nor become dependent on resources outside itself, either of personnel or funds. There were some issues causing tension and some degree of ambivalence, particularly in matters ecumenical, but the Church was confident enough, having experienced the ex-China influx, to welcome missionaries from an even wider range. During this period, apart from those in schools, EP missionaries mostly worked at local congregational level, Chinese and English speaking, or in tasks relating to the whole church to which the Synod appointed them.

The last 25 years, 1972-1997

Regarding South Fujian and East Guangdong, from the time of the missionary withdrawal in 1950-1951, there was no contact with the church in those areas for thirty years. When it came, with China's new 'open' policy it was in the form of personal letters from former Chinese colleagues to their missionary friends. Usually in response to such letters personal visits have been made but there has been no attempt to establish any official link with the Churches. Those who have had the joy and privilege of visiting have marvelled at the numerical growth of the churches, the amazing number and size of new church buildings, the variety of activities involving all ages, the extent of lay training and the increasing number of younger theologically well trained pastors. In the Swatow (Shantou) area the continuity in the church leadership from before the missionaries left to this renewal of contact was especially noticeable, and most clearly represented by the Revd. Zheng Shaohuai (Sheffield Cheng). Above all there is a warm welcome and a most impressive hopefulness in the church's outlook. The full story of the years of silence has yet to be written but we know enough to be able to give thanks for the faithful work and witness of both missionaries and Chinese Christians over the past 150 years.

The Presbyterian Church in Taiwan has grown in a variety of ways, and not least in the number of overseas Taiwanese congregations, from Brazil to Mauritius, from North America to Europe. It has grown like the rest of the country, in wealth, but also in its concern for social and political issues. Its institutions, hospitals, schools and theological colleges have a high reputation, it includes all classes in its membership and continues to be the largest Protestant church in the island. The 'Kaohsiung incident' and the four years imprisonment of its highly respected general secretary, Dr C M Kao, have strengthened its determination to struggle for human rights, and it increasingly identifies itself with the aspirations of the Taiwanese people. It has proved an active member of the WCC and the Council for Word Mission.

Since 1975 the Presbyterian Churches in Singapore and Malaysia have been independent of each other, but their areas of development are not dissimilar. Both have benefitted from a long period of political stability and the remarkable economic progress of the two countries. Both have established new congregations and preaching stations, most often on the initiative of strong congregations, working on the 'daughter churches' principle. In some cases this has also applied to their 'foreign missions' projects. Both have seen spectacular growth in the number and membership of English-speaking congregations, and also of the use of Mandarin in the Chinese. Where necessary they have also made provision for worship services in other languages. In Singapore there has been more opportunity for educational institutions and the churches and school boards have been able to meet the challenge of the government to continual improvement. The loyal support of former pupils has been noteworthy. The Synod there has also responded to the needs of a changing society with its Presbyterian Welfare Services. In social services there has been wide co-operation with other Christian bodies. Within its own life, varying theological traditions have proved more enriching than divisive. The Gereja Presbyterian Malaysia has recently completed a successful sale of the coconut estate at Pontian. This estate was originally bought with Chinese, not Mission, money in the years following the second world war, and its sale has provided the Malaysian Church with capital funds it never previously enjoyed. Even more remarkable, in 1997, the band of the 1st Johore Bahru Company of the Boys Brigade, attached to the Holy Light Presbyterian Church, became the first BB band to visit China and perform in Beijing as part of Children's Day celebrations.

In both Churches the balance of power continues to favour the congregations rather than the central organisation. But both are now Churches with a greater Singapore and Malaysian identity, with deeper roots and growing self-confidence.

The fifth 'field' of England Presbyterian Mission

As guilt over slavery was one factor in the origin of the modern missionary movement, and a sense of shame for the opium trade inspired a desire to share the Gospel in China, so did the Indian Mutiny help arouse the Christian conscience to take more responsibility for British presence in the sub-continent. The work of Alexander Duff had always appealed to Presbyterians north and south of the Border, and it was a product of that work and agent of the Free Church of Scotland's mission in Calcutta, the Revd Behari Lal Singh, who was asked to undertake the task of starting missionary work on behalf of the Presbyterian Church in England. The area chosen was the district of Rajshahi, its main town Rampur Boalia, 170 miles north of Calcutta, and one with which members of the home church had trading links in silk and indigo - a case of the Gospel following trade. At that time, 1862, it had a mixed population of Hindus, mostly land-owners and professional men, Moslems, 85% of the population, and tribal partly nomadic folk. Behari Lal Singh and Mrs Singh began by opening schools, for both boys and girls, and combined this in the dry season with outdoor preaching and distribution of Bibles and tracts. The promised European missionary did not arrive during his twelve years of service. For three years after his death Mrs Singh carried on three of the schools and the orphanage they had begun, and a small Christian community existed by the time the first EP missionary, Dr Donald Morison and his wife arrived in 1878.

From its beginning, through educational, medical or social work and throughout all political changes, the constant theme and continuing thread has been to provide a Christian presence. That was maintained not by visible success of numerical growth but by the patient labours of some remarkable men and women missionaries, always seeking to respond positively to new challenges. They were always understaffed and often felt to be living under the threat that the home church would either close the work down or transfer it to some other mission body. Hospitals were opened but closed, promising developments among both Moslem and aboriginal communities came to an end through lack of staff, both missionary and Bengali, orphanages came into existence but fear of educating the children to a life of dependence on the Mission brought their closure. But in times of crisis such as the cholera epidemic of 1903 or the great famine of 1943 the Christian presence provided by the Mission staff and local Christians was very visible. The early women's work of Mrs Singh and Mrs Morison was maintained and developed in various forms such as the Bolunpur Girls School and Women's Hospital in Rajshahi. The Westminster Hostel, opened in 1926, provided a successful experiment of Hindus and Moslems living together through years of intense communal tension.

The congregation of the church at Rajshahi drew many of its members from those employed in the mission institutions, a source of concern to both missionaries and home church alike. Dr Robert Morison, a son of the first Rajshahi missionary, carried responsibility for both medical work and district evangelism, being ordained by the United Church of North India to which the Rajshahi Church belonged. In 1932 Priya Barui, a school headmaster, after taking theological examinations, was ordained pastor of that church, and thus began his more than forty years of valued service.

The twenty-five years from 1947 to 1972, of which Reg Fenn provides a full account, coincide at the beginning with the partition of India and Pakistan in 1947 and at the end with the emergence, from the traumas of civil war, of the independent state of Bangladesh in 1971-1972.

1947 was also the year of the EP Mission Centenary and at the Assembly in that year, Alan Macleod, on furlough from Bengal, made a challenging appeal to the whole denomination for greater support of this part of its work. Staff was increased and because partition had removed the main purpose of the Westminster Hostel, it was decided to recondition it to provide a hospital for men and women in place of the former medical work in the mission compound. During the next twenty-five years the new hospital's steady development included new women's and children's wards, a nursing school which ultimately received government recognition and the appointment in the late 1950s of its first Bengali superintendent, Dr Upen Malakar. Other changes in the mission compound allowed for the development of a Girls' High School, evidence of the Mission's continuing commitment to education in place of the former primary school. Work among the Santal tribal people developed rapidly after the founding of the first congregation in 1949. As they changed from their traditional nomadic life to one of more settled communities the Mission sought in practical ways to help them in the process. But in any time of political, communal and social unrest, so often lacking the security of a stake in the land, they were most likely to be affected. The 1960s were such a period, graphically described by David Morgan in his 'Memories' and culminating in the civil war between East and West Pakistan which brought Bangladesh to painful birth.

What about the years which have followed, from 1972 to 1997? After being part of the Church of Pakistan and before that of the United Church of North India, both of which had a strong, though distant Presbyterian constituency, this old EP mission field is now the larger part of the Rajshahi deanery of the Church of Bangladesh. This Church embraces two traditions of Anglicanism, CMS and Oxford Mission, as well as this smaller proportion of former Presbyterians. Belonging to a united church, even though it does not include the biggest Protestant denomination, the Baptists, opens up new resources of leadership and reduces the feeling of isolation. In addition to developing its previous institutions and Santal work the succession of devastating floods and famine in recent years have required the Church to play a still greater part in being an ark of hope, rebuilding damaged communities through a programme of visiting, care and practical aid, reconstructing houses, sinking wells, restocking fish and comparable agricultural projects. The active participation of the Church of Bangladesh in the Council for World Mission has also opened up wider horizons for training and service.

The title of the centenary history *Working His Purpose Out* was chosen by the author in the immediate aftermath of the second world war. But neither Band nor anyone else could have foreseen the events of the next

Pilgrims in Mission   *From 1847 to 1997*

few years. Of the three China fields into which English Presbyterians had channelled at least 80% of their missionary effort, only Taiwan remained. The missionary withdrawal from China had also raised many questions regarding the whole missionary enterprise as well as drastically narrowing the areas of the home church's concern. On the other hand, in the short term it had enabled more staff to be appointed and contribute to the development of work in Taiwan, Singapore/Malaysia and East Pakistan, as well as sparing some to other mission bodies. But there was a growing concern to have a wider involvement and to explore new relationships outside the traditional patterns and areas. Links were established with the Presbyterian Churches in Ghana and support provided for Ghanaian chaplaincy work in Britain. Two members of staff were appointed to the Vellore Hospital in India, and a fraternal link was made with one of the Presbyterian Churches in Korea which did not involve personnel or grants but represented on both sides a desire to outgrow traditional patterns. By the time the United Reformed Church was formed and EP mission work became integrated with the Council for Word Mission there was a movement underway to make sure that both the new Church and the Council should carry forward the lessons which had been learned. So now, fifty years on, and with the benefit of hindsight, the title still seems wonderfully appropriate.

Christian Mission Hospital, Rajshahi

THE ENGLISH PRESBYTERIAN MISSION WITHDRAWAL FROM CHINA

All Christian mission bodies, Protestant and Catholic alike, felt the withdrawal or expulsion of their missionaries from China as a major disaster, but for the Presbyterian Church of England it was more than that. Apart from the China Inland Mission no other mission body had been so largely focussed upon China, in which 80% of its mission resources, human, financial, and motivation had been invested. While other mission bodies could appeal for their work in other parts of the world, interpreting events in China in a wider perspective, for English Presbyterians there was no such option. And the very fact of overseas mission being the responsibility of a committee of the Church and not that of an independent society, meant that this was a blow to the whole body of the denomination. Five years previously, in the last few months of the war in the west, a V2 rocket had wiped out most of the denomination's senior officers; now it seemed the rapid change of events in China was doing the same to the recently celebrated hundred years of overseas mission.

From the Tang dynasty onwards, since the year 635 when Christian mission began, there had been other occasions when it was terminated. Throughout the era of Protestant mission, beginning with Robert Morrison in 1807, there had been local attacks on both missionaries and Chinese Christians, and for some the martyrs of the Boxer Rising were still a living memory. More recently, in the 1920s there had been a mass evacuation of missionaries from the interior, leaving only about 500 in the coastal areas. Our English Presbyterian fields of South Fujian and East Guangdong had had their share of local danger and temporary evacuation, most recently as a result of the war with Japan. But all this seemed to bear little comparison with this enforced withdrawal which took place in little more than eighteen months and for most EP missionaries in half that time

I have tried elsewhere *(Neither Bang Nor Whimper)* to give an account and interpretation of the whole picture of the Protestant missionary withdrawal from China, but the size of the canvas and its subject did not allow much space for any details of our own EP Mission experience. At the time it happened, few details appeared in print, mainly out of concern to avoid any possible repercussions in China. The major changes affecting the Church in China, intensified by the Korean War, were followed by the end of any communication, a virtual blackout of reliable church news, national or local. In the light of the unprecedented scale of the withdrawal it seemed more important to all mission boards to address the question *why* rather than *how* it had happened. It was a time for self-criticism, ironically a term popularised in China, and in the minds of some to cast doubt upon the whole mission enterprise, not just in China. Was it doomed from the beginning because of its unavoidable links with western imperialism, exemplified too often, it was suggested, in the outlook, behaviour, policies and methods of the missionaries? In this case there were no dramatic heroics, no missionary martyrs to draw attention away from such awkward questions. And where was God in all this? Was he acting in judgment ?

Rather than engaging directly in this debate, most EP missionaries 'on deputation' were more concerned to stress the fact that despite their withdrawal or the impossibility of return, the Church was there, and to describe it as they knew it. But in the absence of information and any other links for a period of thirty years, it has only been possible with historical hindsight to discern the hand of God and the wisdom of God in what happened, the development of a truly Chinese Church. Sadly, those who had given the greater part of their lives to the Church in China did not survive to share that discovery. For them, retirement years were not a time of continuing links with former friends and colleagues in the places where they had served - as they have been for so many who have written their 'Memories'. for this book— but rather years of silence, questioning, wondering, praying. For some who shared the experience of those years but are now able to look back in thanksgiving, the withdrawal from China will always be a decisive moment in their missionary pilgrimage. For all who are committed to mission now but prepared to learn from the past the 'China experience' provided a catalyst for change and a watershed in mission studies. It both anticipated and precipitated many of the questions and debate that followed about the selfhood of the church and mission - especially western mission - in the context of history. For reasons such as these I believe it is worth recording, as best as I can, a corporate memory of those days as experienced by the last generation of EP missionaries in China..

Civil War renewed

In China the war between Nationalists (KMT) and Communists (CCP) had resumed in July 1947, following the abortive attempts of General Marshall and others to broker a peace settlement. At that time the EP missionaries in South Fujian and Lingdong were more concerned with the immediate problems on their doorsteps than with a war which was being waged in the north, nearly 2000 miles away. By then most of the institutions which had been closed or evacuated during the time of the Japanese occupation were open again. Churches were being rebuilt, with some mission help but more coming from overseas Chinese with whom there had always been close links. Church life was functioning as normally as sky-high inflation would allow. In 1948 that inflation reached a point of three million Chinese dollars to one Hong Kong dollar before it was replaced by another currency which soon went the same way. That proved a strong factor, possibly the last straw, in the Nationalist Government losing popular support.

South Fujian and Lingdong

Although the main fighting was still a long way distant, some parts of both fields were unsettled. And here it is worth drawing attention to a remarkable similarity between the South Fujian and Lingdong mission fields. Both had a major port, Amoy and Swatow, in which there was a sizeable foreign community, both had a Fu (prefecture) city, a centre of Chinese traditional culture, Chuanchow, north of Amoy, and Chao-an (Chao-zhou) north of Swatow. Both had a southern area which had experienced more than its fair share of previous conflict and disturbance, Changpu, south of Amoy, and Swabue at the southern end of the Lingdong field. And both had a large mountainous area which had traditionally been more unsettled, areas in which the remnants of earlier communist activity in the 1920s still survived along with local bandits. In the Lingdong field this extended throughout a large part of the Hakka-speaking areas, and into the Hakka presbytery's own mission field in Jiangsi province. The decision in 1947 to appoint Bob and Joan Elder to work in Shanghang, far up the Han River, and to re-open the mission compound there, closed for many years, is evidence of the optimism of this period. With this part of the Lingdong field may be compared the mountainous area around Yungchun in South Fujian which was also unsettled. In addition to the activities of the local bandits and guerrillas there was also a memory of communist activity in the 1920s, the mass slaughter associated with Peng Pai and the first Chinese Soviet in the Haifeng (Swabue) area; of Zhou En-lai's administration in Swatow during the period of the United Front, and the temporary communist occupation of Swatow following the Nanchang Rising. Only twenty years had passed but memories were still fresh, although rarely mentioned.

War comes nearer

By the summer of 1948 we were much more aware of what was happening on the war front. At Soochow the Church of Christ in China, of which South Fujian and Lingdong Synods were both part, held its first General Assembly since before the Sino-Japanese war began, but attendance of some members from north China was affected. Those in the same year attending the Nanjing conference of the National Christian Council spent a lot of time discussing the right slogan for a new forward movement but also heard the experiences of missionaries living in areas of open warfare. The Scots and Irish Presbyterians in Manchuria were already in that process of agonising decision-making which was to be repeated all over China. In 1947 they had already faced the prospect of being in communist controlled territory, and recommended to their home boards that missionaries who felt they should withdraw in the face of that prospect should be free to do so, with the possibility of being seconded to other work. They also advised against more missionaries being sent to Manchuria 'in the meantime'. In May, 1948 they reaffirmed their intention to stay except for those advised on medical or specific grounds to withdraw (specific grounds to include closure of institutions or forced cessation of work), but before the end of that same month they felt the time had come to reduce their numbers. Plans were made for some to remain but those who left were advised 'to seek temporary work in other parts of China in the hope of returning to Manchuria when the opportunity presents itself'. Among missionaries whose hopes and plans had so often been thwarted, the uncertainty continued about what was temporary or permanent. But they set a precedent, which others were happy to follow, that whatever the Foreign Office or the more over-protective, sometimes authoritarian, members of the home boards might say, the final decision on withdrawal had to remain with those on the field. For those who remained in Mukden (Shenyang) the entry of communist forces on 2nd November, 1948, focussed all attention on the behaviour of the new rulers and their attitude to the church and missionaries.

Dorothy Crawford, one of the Irish Presbyterians previously working in Manchuria, a survivor of the Nagasaki internment camp and second atomic bomb, was one of several from that field who found temporary employment in other parts of China. She came to Lingdong and was appointed to work in the newly-reopened Pue-li Theological College at Chao-an, where she was also joined by Mr and Mrs Kung, refugee teachers from Mukden. In Swatow, two Baptist Missionary Society staff, Dr Nancy Bywaters and Miss Edith Maltby, a nurse, appointed to Xian, now in the war zone, were temporary but very welcome additions to the staff of the Swatow Mission Hospital. The Yule family, from the Presbyterian Church in Australia, were 'marooned' in Amoy by the fortunes of war on their journey northwards. These personal links brought the war nearer, and the sudden takeover of the civilian airports by the Nationalist forces in Taiwan, only 100 miles across the straits made it all the closer.

No longer *if* but *when*

By January, 1949, Manchuria, Shandong, Beijing and a large part of north China, were under communist control. Mao Tse-tung predicted total victory within a year and the People's Liberation Army was already pressing on towards Nanjing, the former Nationalist capital now transferred to Canton. Between September, 1948, and January 1949, one and a half million of Chiang's troops had been killed, captured or changed sides. Earlier speculation that the communists would need to consolidate, at least temporarily before further advance, and that China might have one more experience of division between north and south, was banished by the capture of Nanjing in April and of Shanghai in May. From now on it was only a question of *when* not *if* they would arrive. It also increased, if that were possible, concern to hear what had or was happening in those areas already 'liberated'. Generally speaking, there were favourable reports of the behaviour of the Red Army troops and these were contrasted with those of the KMT. Many of the latter passed through South Fujian and Lingdong as they made to Amoy and Swatow from where they embarked for Taiwan. For those of military age there was real danger of being seized to fill up the ranks of the retreating Nationalist forces. One alternative which many young people took was to disappear into the hills and increase the number of the local communist sympathisers, now preparing to play their part in the coming take-over.

Lingdong, Summer, 1949.

Although local conditions became increasingly unsettled during the first half of 1949, normal church life continued. A major conference of nearly two hundred Chinese and missionary church workers, both those of the Lingdong Synod of the CCC and the equally strong Lingdong Baptist Convention was held at Kakchieh, opposite Swatow, in July, 1949. At its end, between twenty and thirty of them, including a number of missionaries travelled back to the Hakka area together, some of the missionaries planning to spend their summer holiday in Thaiyong, among the hills beyond Wukingfu. White troops, contrary to regulations, joined the civilian passenger launch on which they travelled, and they all became an easy target for a small boat manned by Reds. By the time the launch had been beached and the Whites made their escape, two hours of sporadic firing had been experienced. None of the church workers had been hit but other civilians on the launch were not so fortunate; two were killed and five wounded. There was growing uncertainty about which area was under whose control, and the ending of such uncertainty was a welcome prospect

For the past twenty-five years the mountainous area beyond Wukingfu had always had a fair number of those usually described as 'bandits' but by now locally recognised as 'reds' in contrast to the 'white' Nationalists. During these months Whites and Reds alternately occupied Wukingfu. The missionaries there included Freda Starkey and Jessie Gilchrist. who had gone through a more dangerous experience in 1925 at the hands of KMT troops and barely escaped with their lives. Now, with George and Muriel Mobbs, they had to tread the tight rope of neutrality. Ramsay Chang, headmaster of the Christian Middle School in Wukingfu, was blacklisted by the Whites for keeping the school open during Red occupation of the area, and had to hide in the Mobbs' house till they had withdrawn.

In November, 1948, the new currency 'broke' and many Chinese who had converted their Hong Kong dollars into the new currency lost a lot of money. The drawn-thread work industry which played such an important part in the church's finances was particularly affected because of its Hong Kong links and several leading laymen were made bankrupt. In spite of the combined political, military, social and economic confusion, the 'business as usual' attitude in the life of the Church and its institutions as well as of the missionaries continued. A new ministerial missionary, Peace Montgomery and his wife Mary, had come in November, 1948, and in March, 1949, two new doctors arrived, Peter Shave and his wife Margaret to serve in Swatow, and Arthur Farmer for Wukingfu. Within his first two weeks the latter had been taken ten miles to the local communist H.Q. to attend the wife of one of the officials, 'It was of obvious importance to keep on good terms with them'. In June, Tony Strange, the superintendent of the Swatow Mission Hospital, took his nine year old son, John, with him when he travelled two days by sea launch to visit the Swabue Hospital and assess its work and prospects. By then communist guerrillas already controlled most of the

Swabue hinterland.

In September, 1949, the Church had planned to celebrate the centenary of its history but by then the expectation of an early 'liberation' and the reluctance of most people to be away from home at such a time caused a temporary postponement. In Swatow large numbers of nationalist soldiers were making demands on the Hospital, including admission as in-patients. A new class of twenty nurses was enrolled. An older mission house had been divided into two, one of them occupied by the Shaves but neither water nor plumbing was as yet installed. At a Mission Council meeting held in October it was agreed that all property being used by the Church, including the Hospital, should be handed over to it but that mission houses should remain the property of the Mission.

'Liberation'

Sometimes the missionaries were dependent on the BBC for information of what was happening and on October 12th Tony Strange wrote, 'I have just heard from London that troops are evacuating Swatow, and that the Communists are 45 miles from Canton. This time the BBC is accurate about Swatow. The troops are leaving for Formosa, and during the last three days have been roaming the streets acting as "Press Gangs", seizing men to drag them off to Formosa to make up their depleted army numbers. In addition they have been seizing small boats......It is only 8 p.m. but the streets are deserted, and last night and today a lot of men from the foreshore have come into the Compound to hide from the Press Gangs. Shops are mostly shuttered with doors just a little ajar, and coolies have disappeared from the waterfront'.

[Twelve days later, October 24th, Swatow was 'liberated'. The event is described in a letter from Tony Strange, quoted by Margaret Strange in her 'Memories' on pages 59-62].

Early reactions

The Lingdong missionaries were agreed in finding the first six months following 'liberation' a great relief from the former uncertainty, and also more hopeful than they had expected. In each place where they lived, Swatow, Chao-an, Swabue, Wukingfu and Shanghang, it had been peaceful. The experience in each was comparable with that described in Swatow; and they welcomed the early decision of the British Government to recognise the People's Republic of China. In Chao-an the Women's School and the Pue-li Theological College had both taken in new classes. Both of these schools had Chinese women as principals, Miss Huang and Miss Lim, and the missionaries kept well in the background as these two outstanding colleagues coped with visits and questioning by the new authorities. Christmas that year was celebrated with great enthusiasm and a memorable open air performance of the Christmas story drew a vast crowd and fascinated attention from the many 'comrades' who watched it. In Swatow the churches were full and each had a large number of additions to membership.

Blockade

In such conditions, Tony and Margaret Strange were able to have a holiday in Wukingfu at the beginning of January, 1950, leaving their children in Swatow with their friends in the American Baptist Mission, Carl and Louise Capen. But soon after their return the blockade imposed by the KMT, already causing a lot of unemployment in the coastal area, took a more dangerous turn, with a series of air-raids from Taiwan. A bomb demolished a row of five houses in a street next to the Compound. Two successive days brought three raids a day, and one day a Liberator bombed for over an hour 'but all the bombs dropped in the sea'. (*In the light of subsequent events they may have been mining the entrance to the harbour*) The Swatow port authorities then closed the port to daylight shipping. Consequently in March, when Beth Hood had to return home to look after her mother, incapacitated by a stroke, she had to seize the right moment from a tossing sampan to clamber up the side of a ship in the middle of the harbour - and in the middle of the night.

The mission staff in Wukingfu now comprised Freda Starkey, Jessie Gilchrist, George Mobbs and Arthur Farmer. Although in February, 1950, the last named obtained a permit to visit Hong Kong to marry his fiancee and return, he could not get a permit to bring her back with him. Both had to live with this painful separation until October when the OMC approved his leaving China, but even then he did not get his exit permit until January, 1951. Jim Waddell was more fortunate. He had been on furlough at the time Swabue was 'liberated' but was able to return there from Hong Kong in the way described in his letter on pages 63-64.

Leaving and getting back

Although there were signs that future entry permits might be difficult to obtain, the furlough plans made at the Mission Council meeting in February were mainly determined by the usual considerations of maintaining the work, the normal five year term of service, and family circumstances. It was agreed that Ruth Milne should go from July, 1950, for eight months, and returning enable Tony Strange to be away from April, 1951, to April, 1952, and that Margaret Strange should take their children, John and Anne, in June, so that John might enter Eltham College in the autumn. George Hood would complete his five year term in June. In May he sought the views of his colleagues on whether he should stay longer but was advised to take his furlough when due, with a view to getting back to China as soon as possible. Eventually, in May, Ruth Milne, Margaret Strange and the children, along with the Principal of the Pue-li Theological College, Lim Zuat Hi, sailed out of Swatow during the hours of darkness on the ill-fated 'Anhui', the last British ship to leave Swatow for many weeks. Before doing so they had completed what was now the normal procedure of announcing their intended departure in the press, in case anyone had a claim against them, and then waiting for ten days or a fortnight to get their exit permits.

Korean War

George Hood went through all these procedures and was booked on the next sailing of the 'Anhui' to Hong Kong in June. Unfortunately it struck a mine as it entered Swatow harbour. The explosion put it out of commission and resulted in the port being closed to shipping. George had to re-negotiate his exit permit to travel by land. On the day before he left by bus on a week's journey to the Hong Kong border, we heard on the BBC that war had broken out in Korea.

South Fujian, similarities and a major difference

The experience of the South Fujian missionaries was not much different from those in Lingdong except in one important way. The missionaries in Chuanchow, Ian and Joyce Latto, Wenona Jett, Kathleen Duncan, the Landsboroughs, Tunnells and Shorts reported a peaceful takeover both there and in Yungchun on August 31st, 1949. But whereas in Lingdong. Swatow had been abandoned by the nationalists without a fight, fighting around Amoy and the exchange of artillery fire delayed its 'liberation' by nearly six weeks. Two letters from Robert Tully, included in the 'Memories' (pages 56-59) describe the siege conditions at Amoy and the island of Kulangsu. In October, 1949, the Amoy Committee, acting on behalf of the Mission Council (no communications were possible with Chuanchow) agreed that wives with children should leave, namely Joyce Beeby with two small children and Mrs Yule with three, and that Dan Beeby should also 'proceed on furlough so that after a period at home he will be available to relieve others'. The departure of the Beebys on the 'Anhui' at the end of October was not without incident. The ship came under fire which killed three and wounded twenty-three of those on board. As a trained nurse Joyce Beeby was able to assist a doctor in tending the wounded. That was the last ship to leave Amoy before the communist occupation of the port, and the subsequent blockade by the Taiwan-based nationalists. At a later date, word came that foreigners leaving China would be required to make their exit through Tientsin, Shanghai or Canton, each of which would require long, expensive and stressful journeys for the missionaries in South Fujian and Lingdong. Fortunately it was not consistently implemented.

Restrictions

In both areas the missionaries were coming to terms with the limited movement allowed but fretful at the resultant limitation on their usefulness. Ian Latto reported home that bicycles were being registered and that the form to be completed was the same for bicycles, pedicabs, rickshaws and motorcars. It could also be said that foreigners were being treated the same as anyone else. In this case , 'Each applicant states the make and age of his bicycle, his driving experience, his occupation, use to which the bicycle is put, his parents' occupation, and has a guarantor to be responsible for the misuse of the vehicle'. In Kulangsu Robert Tully found himself in the embarrassing position of being an unofficial diplomatic go-between. At this stage and for many years to come, in spite of the British desire to establish what they saw as normal diplomatic relations, it was not reciprocated on the Chinese side. Consequently the British consul in Amoy was not recognised. Tully wrote home in May, 1950, 'There is still no consular recognition and several times when the authorities want something they get round the difficulty by getting someone to speak to me and I then speak to the consul! It is very awkward being drawn into things'.

In the UK the attitude was still cautiously optimistic, exemplified in the action of the newly appointed OM Secretary, Tim Healey, in July, 1950, arranging for the dispatch of a church bell to Shanghang, as requested and commissioned by Bob Elder.

The Government's challenge to the Church - The Manifesto

But from April onwards, significant changes were developing in China. Church leaders had sought a meeting in Beijing with government in the hope of clarifying the implementation of its religious policy, including the future of missionaries. But the meeting which ensued with Premier Zhou Enlai became the occasion at which the conditions for the churches having any place at all in the New China were spelt out in uncompromising terms. The onus was on them to prove their loyalty and carry out the Three-Self principles. So far as missionaries were concerned it appeared likely that they would have to leave the country when their visas or passports expired, and that re-entry would be limited to those who had a demonstrable contribution to make to the New China. While church and other Christian leaders wrestled with the implications of this policy no official report was immediately forthcoming. It was not until June that Tully sent home some account of the Manifesto which did not take its final form until July. It was only published in the August 19th issue of *Tian Feng*, and did not receive its final endorsement until the biennial meeting of the National Christian Council, October 18th to 25th. During these six months of uncertainty, intensified by the outbreak and unpredictable effect of the Korean War, Tully and his colleagues were locked in discussions over property matters with the South Fujian Synod and the boards of various related institutions. These were complicated by the three-sided partnership with the London Missionary Society and Reformed Church in America as well as the varying conditions in Kulangsu, Amoy, Chuanchow, Yungchun and Changpu.

OMC decision re Mission-held property

In Swatow the Lingdong Synod Secretary, the Revd Sheffield Cheng (Zheng Shaohuai) had the confidence in these matters of both the missionaries on the spot and the OM Committee in London. In response to a letter of August 24th, the OM Secretary had cabled to the missionaries both in South Fujian and Lingdong, 'At your discretion Committee prepared consider unconditional transfer all rights and responsibilities in all, repeat all, property to Synod for Church use'. But it became clear by October that custodianship rather than total transfer was to be the way forward. Sheffield Cheng gave the reasons briefly, '(1) There are yet no official regulations regarding the transfer of foreign property; (2) Consequently no property can be sold to meet land tax that is reported to be rather high; (3) Practically all mission fields seem agreed about this arrangement, with the consequence that the Church of Christ in China General Assembly have decided to ask all churches to do it this way'. And with his letter he enclosed a copy of the proposed form of agreement between owner and custodian.

Land tax dilemma

With ownership remaining in the hands of the sending church, and only custodianship transferred, Cheng admitted that responsibility for land tax would rest on the Church in England rather than the Synod. He pointed out that because the Synod was committed to an annual decrease in funding to achieve full self-support in five years, there need not be an increase in the total annual grant. Within the next four months all these calculations had been overtaken by events, and in early 1951 by the end of normal grants and communication. The issue of responsibility for land tax for the year 1950 remained a matter of debate. In the end, without accepting responsibility the OMC made an ex gratia payment equivalent to the sum required and the matter was finally closed. In all these property matters there was no reluctance on the part of the OMC to transfer rights and ownership to the appropriate body in China, normally the relevant Synod. But the contemporary experience of British commercial firms, the sums they had been required to pay on various grounds, and the fear that the granting of exit permits might be affected was always a cause for anxiety. For the church in China, facing an uncertain future and the requirement of self-support, paying land tax was an intolerable burden to contemplate.

Missionaries' return?

Regarding missionaries the Lingdong Synod remained optimistic about their future service. Before leaving on furlough in the middle of 1950 both Ruth Milne and George Hood had been invited to return, and in August the invitation was repeated in a letter from the Synod Secretary. That same month the Synod was asked by the Swatow Mission Council to consider the return of missionaries individually, but it was not until December that the Synod replied verbally that any who felt they should stay would be welcome to do so, and the invitation to George and Ruth to return still stood; all of this despite the reports coming out of the Beijing meeting.

Impact of Korean War

During the second half of 1950 the Three-self principle became overtly political. Patriotic feelings of hostility were focussed on the USA, both for its actions over Korea and for stationing its Seventh Fleet between the mainland and Taiwan to deter any attack upon the latter. The watchword of the Three-Self Reform Movement had now the added words, 'Oppose America Aid Korea'. When American forces in the UN Command under General Macathur crossed the 38th Parallel into North Korea on October 8th, and three weeks later reached the Yalu River, the border with China, Beijing declared this a threat to national security. Chinese troops engaged South Korean troops later that month south of the Yalu River; on November 26th they launched a major attack and drove the UN forces back, reaching and crossing the 38th Parallel into South Korea by Christmas.

This was a crisis period in the Cold War and fear of a Third World War was very real. The setbacks in Korea put Truman under pressure to resort to the atom bomb; in China the Korean War was seen as a war of survival for New China and its Revolution. By being part of the UN forces Britain was unofficially at war with China although it was in the interests of both sides not to make it official. But as the danger of open and wider conflict increased, the OM Committee feared that the delays in granting exit permits could mean that some missionaries might be held hostage or interned. The tone of the Manifesto, associating the missionary movement explicitly with imperialism, and now bearing the signatures of a majority of the church leaders and members increased the anxiety. Quite apart from restrictions on their work, it was now clear that missionary presence was more than an embarrassment, it was a danger to the Church. To remain was no longer an option. What might have been a gradual withdrawal now became a hurried exodus

OMC decision to withdraw and Chinese response

When the Overseas Missions Committee met on December 19th, 1950, it resolved to withdraw all its missionaries from China, but it was not until February, 1951, that Healey had opportunity to explain this decision to the whole church in the pages of the *Presbyterian Messenger*. By then it was clearly in the interests of both the Church in China as well as of the missionaries themselves that the withdrawal should be completed as soon as possible. Healey set out the reasons behind the decision. In doing so he quoted in full both the November letter from the Church of Christ in China and the Manifesto, and in the general mood of that time, suggested that the former expressed the true feelings of the Church while the latter gave an idea of the 'atmosphere in which Christians find themselves'. He virtually assumed that all who signed did so under duress. The text of the letter explaining the OMC's decision which had been sent to the General Assembly and to the two Synods of South Fujian and Lingdong in which the missionaries served, was also quoted in full. The following month the March issue of the *Presbyterian Messenger* printed the reply of the General Assembly, dated 27th January, 1951, expressing deep gratitude for past service, and 'sadness because in this stage of transition we may seem to be withdrawing from the ecumenical fellowship which, of course, is not true. The bonds of love and prayer will be as strong as ever even though we receive no aid from you in personnel and funds'. The letter affirmed the decision not to receive any further foreign mission aid, and this decision alone showed how far and how quickly the scene had changed in the previous two months.

Throughout the second half of 1950, Protestant mission boards in London were all concerned with how to interpret the rapidly changing scene in China, and were particularly anxious about the impact on their supporters of the Manifesto, now endorsed by so many well known Chinese Christian leaders. The fact that Healey was the first to grasp the nettle of publishing it is worth noting. Although the English Presbyterian Mission was so China-focussed and therefore so vulnerable to the effects of a withdrawal, in this situation there were advantages in overseas mission being the responsibility of the whole Presbyterian Church of England and not simply of a Society

Final withdrawal from South Fujian.

In South Fujian, by the end of 1950, only the Tunnells and Landsboroughs in Chuanchow and the Tullys in Kulangsu remained. During December the Lattos and their two children, the Shorts with their twins and Kathleen Duncan had made their way via Canton to reach Hong Kong on the 14th. After the usual procedures the Tunnells and the Landsboroughs reached Hong Kong on February 7th, 1951. Writing on February 2nd, from Kulangsu, Robert Tully referred to a meeting held two days previously, 'attended by representatives of all the Kulangsu churches and institutions with which we were connected. Many pleasant things were said and we were given a magnificent banner with the words (*I Cor.15:58*),"Labour in the Lord is not wasted"'. Later in the month he was still dealing with property matters, but finally he and Mrs Tully departed and reached Hong Kong on March 14th,1951.

The final communication to the OMC from the South Fujian Synod was dated February 23rd, 1951:

'Dear Secretary,
We are very glad to receive your letter of January 1st, 1951. We are very much obliged for your kind attention to the South Fukien Synod of the Church of Christ in China. The South Fukien Synod and its associated institutions have decided in the future to run on the plan of full self-support, self-government and self-propagation in the Church so as to establish an autonomous Chinese Christian Church.
We hope that you will pray for us so that our work may be blessed by God and be strengthened by the Holy Spirit in our witness to our Lord and Master, Jesus Christ.
Signed by the Chairman, Chng Haupho
Secretary, Teng Ekkheng

Withdrawal from Lingdong

In the Lingdong area the main exodus of missionaries took place in the first three months of 1951, a period in which land reform was already seriously affecting the rural churches. Accusation meetings were also on the increase against landlords, employers, and those exercising authority in institutions, including schools and hospitals. Contact with missionaries gave grounds for incurring suspicion. Christmas in 1949 had been celebrated with great enthusiasm but a year later the church choir which Peter Shave had been training was told it could only sing if Peter did not conduct. By now the regulations restricting religious activities to church buildings were being enforced and neither preaching in the hospital nor the giving out of religious literature was permitted.

At the end of January, 1951, Arthur Farmer was able to leave and at last join up with his wife Audrey in Hong Kong. Bob and Joan Elder got their exit permits in Shanghang and planned to travel overland. They reached Hong Kong via Canton on February 28th. In February, Jim Waddell and Celia Downward got their exit permits in Swabue, George Mobbs, Freda Starkey and Jessie Gilchrist in Wukingfu, Agnes Richards and Dorothy Crawford in Chao-an. All of these left in March. By the middle of that month only Tony Strange, Peter Shave, Gwen Burt and the Graf family were left in Swatow. Peter Shave left on March 23rd and Tony Strange got news of his permit on Easter Sunday. He had been called for his exit 'interview' in December; it had lasted two hours, and although he had been complimented on the honest way he had answered all the questions, his colleagues were anxious that he might be detained as the chairman of the Mission Council. He himself was increasingly anxious about handing over the hospital because of the reluctance of Chinese staff to be left in charge.

Anxious delays in Swatow

At the end of April only Gwen Burt and the Graf family remained in Swatow. After his arrival in Hong Kong in March, George Mobbs suggested that both of these colleagues had fallen foul of the authorities by arguing too much over matters in which they believed they were in the right. They suffered in consequence. Five months passed before Claire Graf and the children were able to leave, and two months more, November, before Joop Graf arrived in Hong Kong. In Swatow he had been put on the ship under armed escort, after being required to apologise and make some payment to two former employees. For six more weeks Gwen Burt was on her own but finally reached Hong Kong in December, 1951. She had been accused of infringing some currency regulations of which she was unaware, and required to pay a fine of £100.

The last Protestant missionary

One English Presbyterian missionary still remained, but voluntarily, in China. Margaret (Peggy) Eldridge, a qualified pharmacist, had been appointed by the WMA to serve on the staff of Cheloo Christian University in 1948. This university had been temporarily evacuated to central China but returned to Shandong in 1949. She taught there until 1952 when the university was dismembered, and for a further year in the new large medical college which took its place. By this time she had married one of her colleagues, who was half-Chinese. With a mother-in-law and a brother-in-law who were counted as Chinese citizens, she had a unique opportunity to see New China not only through her own eyes, but also through those of her family. She and her husband, Mr Kiesow, left China in September, 1953, for their own personal reasons. They were not required to leave but did so when her services were still appreciated. As well as being the last English Presbyterian missionary to leave China, Margaret Kiesow was the last of any Protestant mission body to do so.

Postscript

The withdrawal of missionaries from mainland China, more quickly than first expected, presented the OMC and WMA with the unusual experience of a missionary surplus. Fortunately there was in Taiwan a church in which the South Fujian missionaries' qualifications, experience and knowledge of that Chinese dialect might be used. Of the South Fujian missionaries Boris and Clare Anderson had already been transferred from Chuanchow to Tainan in 1948. In the same year another new missionary, Kathleen Moody, was appointed, initially to do social work, but soon to find increasingly her special niche in the music department of Tainan Theological College. After the withdrawal from the mainland, by the invitation of the Presbyterian Church in Taiwan, Dan and Joyce Beeby, David and Jean Landsborough, Daisy Pearce and Alvinza Riddoch followed. Christina Holmes, originally appointed to South Fujian but temporarily doing language study in Singapore, was also transferred to Taiwan. All of these were to play a significant part in the development of Tainan Theological College, Changhua Christian Hospital, Kindergarten Teacher Training and Tunghai Christian University.

The redeployment of missionaries to serve in Singapore and Malaysia was more complicated. In the first place it was a much smaller church, a church lacking most of the institutions in which many missionaries in China had been serving, and a church which previously had had very few missionaries. But it was also one in which the South Fujian, Chao-zhou and Hakka dialects were all used. However, in addition to the E.P. missionaries there were others from South Fujian, notably those of the London Missionary Society, with whom some of the Singapore church leaders already had personal links. The LMS had also an earlier historical link with Singapore and Malaysia. In China the LMS had had a major part of its work in Mandarin-speaking areas and naturally hoped to be able to redeploy some of this staff in Singapore and Malaysia. In addition to these two potential sources of missionary staff, there was another, the biggest of them all, the China Inland Mission, soon to be known as the Overseas Missionary Fellowship of the China Inland Mission (OMF). No other body had been so identified in the popular mind with mission work among Chinese - it had no other *raison d'etre* - and consequently it was under great pressure, as quickly as possible to continue work among Chinese, in Taiwan and among the Chinese 'diaspora' in South-east Asia.

In these circumstances the Singapore/Malaya Synod of the Chinese Christian Church took the brave step of welcoming all willing to come. Like other churches in Malaya it saw the creation of the New Villages as an unexpected opportunity for mission, but knew it lacked the personnel to seize it. In the past, in a manner comparable to both British and Indian communities, the Chinese speaking churches had looked to their motherland to provide ministers, preachers and women evangelists. That source was now cut off at the same time as these new sources of missionaries opened up. The overall need of staff, to share in theological training, to promote English-speaking services and education, to stimulate women's, youth and children's work, as well as the special challenge of the New Villages were all on the Synod's agenda. So far as their relations to the Synod were concerned, there was only one major difference among the missionaries: those belonging to the OMF were happy to give help to congregations at a local level, while also pursuing their own mission projects, but did not accept Synod appointment. The remainder did, and also shared in one Mission Council. At one time or another this body included ex-China missionaries of the English Presbyterian Mission, London Missionary Society, Presbyterian Church in Ireland, Church of Scotland, Reformed Church in America, Society of Friends, as well as those directly appointed to Singapore or Malaysia.

Redeployment discussions were held with both the Synod Executive in Singapore and the LMS in London. Out of this developed a close co-operation, represented by a Joint Malaya Group in London and a joint Malaya Mission Coumcil. This reflected the nature of the Church in Singapore and Malaya they were serving, which drew so many of its members from two synods of the Church of Christ in China; and this unity in mission in Singapore and Malaysia pre-dated by many years the unity finally achieved in the formation of the United Reformed Church.

Of the ex-China E.P. missionaries the most senior was Robert Tully from Amoy. He became a valued science teacher in the rapidly developing Presbyterian Boys' School, of which Bernarr Atherton was the new headmaster. All the other ex-China E.P. missionaries came from the Lingdong area. Bob and Joan Elder lived in Ipoh, Bob having accepted a call from the largely expatriate English-speaking congregation there, and were able to help Church Missionary Society work in the Hakka-speaking New Villages of that area. Gwen Burt, Agnes Richards and George and Beth Hood were in Johore state, the first named in Batu Pahat, the second in Kulai alongside Joyce Lovell of the LMS and Mr Lim Kui Chun, the preacher in charge of both Senai and Kulai, and the Hoods in Johore Bahru. Celia Downward was especially associated with the Chao-zhou speaking churches in Singapore but soon became more widely involved in women's work and Sunday School training.

Of the remaining ex-China missionaries, three doctors and their wives, the Farmers, the Shaves and the Tunnells, continued their missionary service at Rajshahi or, seconded to the Welsh Presbyterian Mission, in northeast India.. One other doctor, Ruth Milne gave five years service in Nigeria, seconded to the Church Missionary Society, and Neil Fraser continued his work with the Leprosy Mission in Hong Kong. Of the ministerial missionaries, Jim Waddell served for four years as an Emergency Administration Officer in Malaysia, working in predominantly Chaozhou-speaking New Villages in Province Wellesley, but then rejoined the mission staff to work under the Synod in Singapore. The remaining missionaries resigned, to continue their pilgrimage in mission in the ministry or their professions at home, in other areas of work, or in some cases, their retirement.

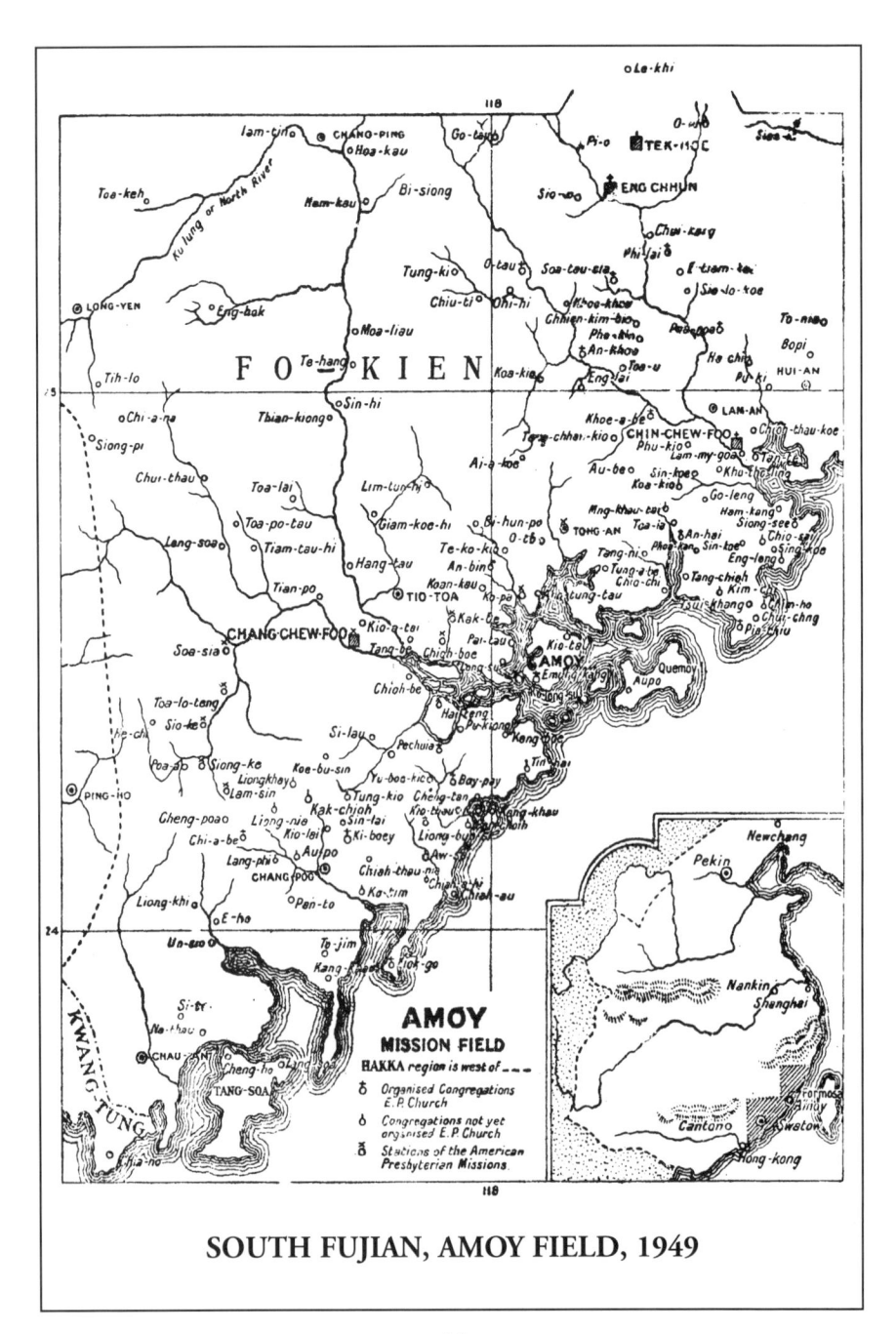

SOUTH FUJIAN, AMOY FIELD, 1949

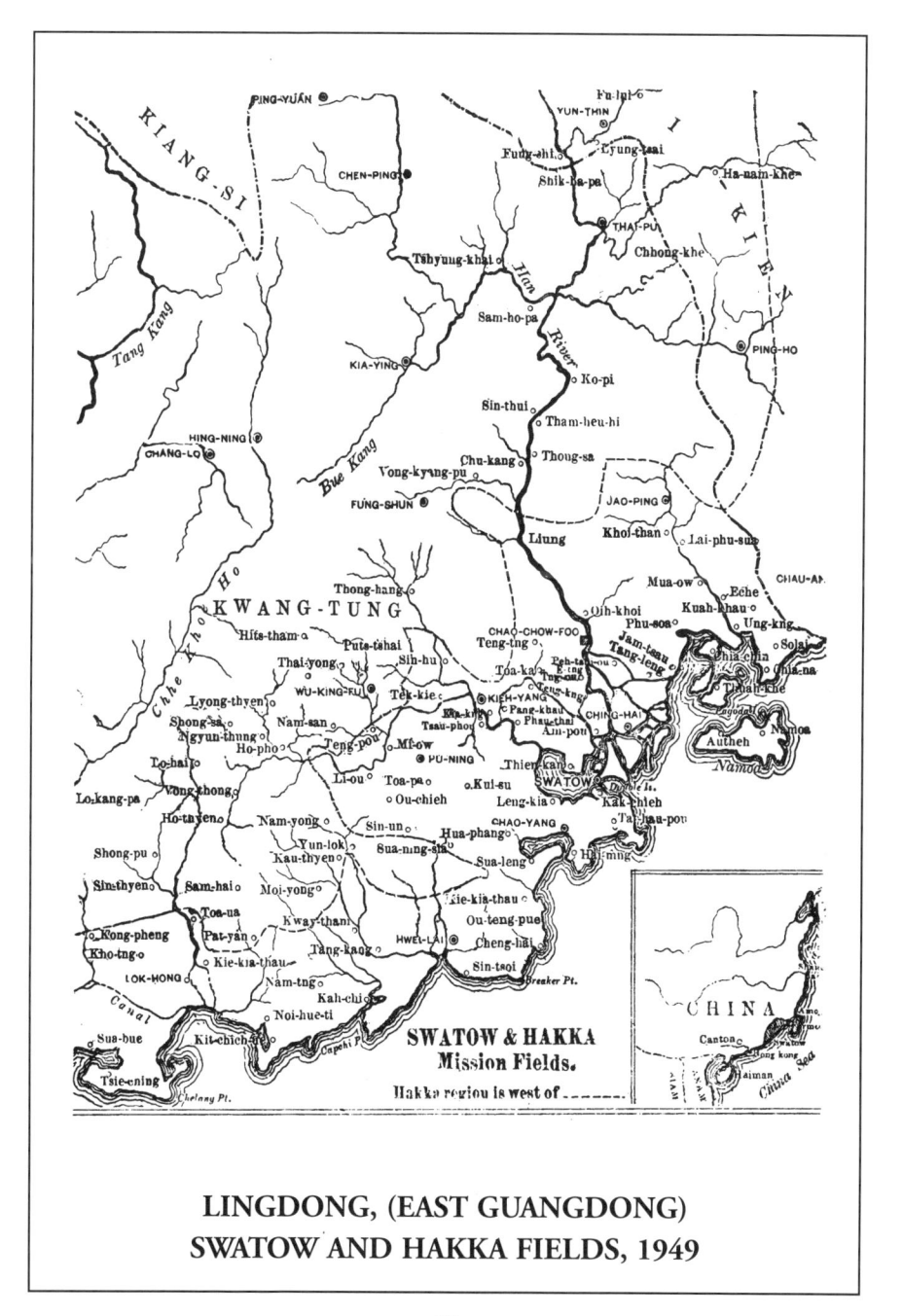

LINGDONG, (EAST GUANGDONG)
SWATOW AND HAKKA FIELDS, 1949

MEMORIES: SOUTH FUJIAN AND LINGDONG

As a trained teacher, followed by two years of missionary training at Carey Hall, Selly Oak, **Celia Downward** *served from 1938 to 1951 in the Swatow field, mostly in the Swabue area. After the withdrawal of missionaries from China she served for a further twenty years in Singapore and Malaysia, as Synod secretary for Women's Work and giving pastoral care to congregations in north-east Malaysia. The following extract from her book, privately printed,* Life in the Land of the Dragon, *describes some of her China experience.*

The Famine Year 1943

In spite of such pleasant happenings clouds began to show on the horizon. Farmers were already fearful because drought was causing the fields to be hard, dry and cracked. It spread throughout the time of the planting of rice and filled their hearts with dread. It was normally a rice growing area but in any time of shortage rice could be imported from Thailand through Swatow. This was now not possible with the Japanese holding the port. Rich farmers and landlords at the first early signs of drought began to buy up all the rice they could and hoard it. Some of the villages along the river managed to plant sweet potatoes and water them with water carried from the river. When famine was inevitable the rich farmers sold very small amounts of rice for disgracefully high prices. The poorer families sold family possessions like mosquito nets, bedding, tools and furniture in order to buy rice if possible. One time when I needed to return to Wukingfu sooner than arranged because I had a fever, probably dengue, I decided to ride pillion on a bicycle but it was a slow journey because the cyclist was weakened by hunger. We came to the top of a hill and looked down on an unusual market. It was where hungry villagers were selling their belongings to help them take a journey to the state where Chiang Kai Shek's son was the governor. This was quite a distance away from the famine area and they had had a harvest. It was not as good as usual so rice was being rationed. When news spread of this harvest many travelled there hoping to get rice. The rationing meant that there was none left for people from other parts. They had to return to their own villages, but bloated with hunger and sick, many died on the return journey. Those who did manage to return had nowhere to live because many had sold even their homes for a song to rich landlords in a desperate venture to go where they believed there would be rice to spare. Now it was a desperate time to travel around the area and I began to see scenes such as I have watched on TV of similar famines in Africa and elsewhere. Each morning there were bodies of people who had died in the night in the market places and the streets.

Once I was in Kityang where 200 children had been picked up early one morning and taken to the Baptist Mission Hospital. It was not that parents had abandoned them but that they had survived longer than their parents . I went into the Hospital where I met a very distressed American doctor. The 200 needy children were lying on straw beds and had been divided into three groups. One group was of those that the doctor and medical staff felt could not possibly recover. A second group needed a lot of care and medicine and still might not get better, and the third with care, food and medicines had a fair chance of recovery. The doctor said, 'I have had to be God and decide which we could save with our meagre resources', for both food and medicines were difficult to buy however much money one might have.

Some aid did eventually arrive from the Red Cross. Then our Chinese friends were troubled how it should be used. Should they concentrate on one village or what? Should they make the rice into gruel and give a bowlful of comfort, for as long as it lasted, to those who came with a bowl to fill? The last suggestion was the one accepted. I arrived at the distribution centre when the distribution was nearly finished. I watched a small girl with her little brother and a bowl having it filled. She took him aside and fed him with the gruel. When it was finished she wiped the inside with her finger and licked her finger. That was all she had. It was an example of older sister taking care of younger brother - but what unbelievable unselfishness. There were other examples of actions seemingly difficult to explain. Girls in one village went out when it was dark to steal the leaves from the tops of sweet potatoes, knowing that if they were caught death would be the punishment.

Conditions prevented my colleagues and myself from doing anything useful and we had no resources to help the distressed so we returned to Wukingfu. I had also been taken ill with malaria. It was decided that I should discontinue my journeys and teach instead in a Church school which had been evacuated there from Swatow at an earlier date. We kept appealing to the Government for help and eventually Red Cross aid did arrive.

Before I began teaching in the School I went into the hills for a rest. We were very fortunate because some of the missionaries in the compound had a very well stocked store cupboard with flour, powdered milk and tins of many kinds of food. They had always kept this store of food in good times. Now we could use it even though there was not enough for a normal diet. News got around and thieves and gangs became active. There was a break-in in the compound. A notice appeared in the village from a magistrate living at a good distance from us. It asked the local people to protect us because we were friends from an Allied Country.

Rumours had already spread that some of us were in Thai Yong, in the hills above Wukingfu. The headman of the village there told us that a bad gang of robbers was planning to kidnap some of us and hold us up for ransom. The price they intended to demand was to be less than the price of a buffalo! There were very few such animals left by then. They had either starved to death or been killed reluctantly for food. When the drought which caused the famine ended, farmers had to pull the plough themselves to break up the parched land and prepare it for rice planting. The Thai Yong village headman advised us to leave. He asked us though that we should not all go together but in twos and threes so that the bandits would not know what was happening. We sent the mothers and children first, but by the third night, those of us who remained gathered together in one bungalow to give each other comfort and courage. We left safely, early the next morning, wondering whether to be insulted, or otherwise, that five of us were only worth the price of a buffalo!

I taught English as a preparation for the pupils hoping to proceed to further education, and Religious Knowledge, but had several bouts of fever and finally a very severe attack of malaria. We had no quinine which was the usual medicine for malaria. Fortunately the doctor working in the hospital had been with the Australian army and had a supply of another drug. That was atabrin which changes the colour of the skin to yellow. The fever was so high that my hair came out until I had quite a big ball of my own hair! By then my furlough was well overdue and another senior missionary had eye trouble and needed to go home. It was a food deficiency disease and gives an indication of the health problems which Chinese friends suffered at the end of the famine.

The famine left many marks on people's lives. Events for some time were dated from 'The famine year', or 'Before the famine' or 'After the famine'.

It was decided that we should take the journey across country to Kunming where there was an airport. The only way to do this was on foot for part of the way and then by a salt lorry. Its engine was worked by the heat of charcoal. It was very hot and dusty. I was sitting by the place where the charcoal was fed into the lorry. When we arrived in Kunming the lines on my face stood out with coal dust in the grooves. We were able to get money from the bank there and tickets on a Chinese plane across the Hump, as the Himalayan mountains were called, into Dum-dum Airport in Calcutta. It was an uncomfortable journey because the plane was not adequately pressurized and there was little oxygen. I must have had a spell of unconsciousness for I wakened with a start when we landed in Calcutta. I must have looked strange anyway for my skin was still yellow after the treatment for malaria. I was also wearing a home-made cotton hat to hide my baldness! I did not mind that for I was on my way home. German U-boats in the Atlantic meant that we had to travel in a convoy of ships, but I arrived home safely and was there for the end of the War in 1945.

Ian Latto *trained for the Presbyterian ministry with a view to missionary service. He was appointed to the Amoy (South Fujian) field and arrived there in 1935. After the missionary withdrawal from China he continued his ministry in the UK, serving congregations at Newbiggin-by-the-Sea, Chorlton-cum-Hardy, Waterloo, Caradoc and Malpas.*

South Fujian Memories 1935 - 1950

Revival meetings frequently occur in my memories. Having arrived in Amoy (Xiamen) in November, 1935, I was posted to Yungchun, one hundred miles to the north-west. When I reached there in January, 1936, a week of such meetings was in progress. The evangelist was Lim Phoe Hian and more than 600 listeners filled the church. He was a forerunner of the more famous Dr John Sung who followed in 1937 and stayed with me during his visit. Dr Sung drew an audience of about 1000, many coming from the surrounding villages and sleeping in the church. He was a dramatic and powerful preacher with a gift for challenging illustrations. Being January the weather was cool and the evening meetings were held in the church, but during the day the people gathered, morning and afternoon, in the school grounds and an awning was erected to protect their heads from the warm sun. These meetings concluded in the formation of preaching bands to carry the message to the neighbouring villages, and in a baptismal service beside the river.

During the first two years, study of the Amoy (South Fujian) dialect on a one-to-one basis predominated, but as I was coming to the end of this period, the Sino-Japanese war began. To prevent the Japanese military vehicles rushing inland, the Chinese destroyed all motor roads within fifty miles of the coast. This made little difference to our work up-country - previously the bus route had ended at Yungchun - but it did mean that supplies of goods were more difficult to obtain and travel to Amoy for Mission Council meetings took several days. Ours was a rural area, self-supporting in rice, and able to supply a surplus to the coastal area. Apart from the pottery works at Tehwa, north of Yungchun, the only other industry was that of a few very small cigarette and clothing factories.

Among the people of that time I remember Luke, a simple soul, once employed by missionaries. He suffered from a bad leg but in spite of this walked several *li* (three *li* to a mile) to church. After the service he would come to my house to report on the leg and have a word of prayer. Above his village he had a place of prayer where he would pray for the godless among his neighbours. But one week he reported he had kept clear of it. A pressed circle of grass showed that a tiger had slept there.

During a vacancy of the Khoe-sia church, the village primary school headmaster, Mr Li, moved the school into the church. When the new pastor, Pastor Tan, was appointed, Mr Li resented being forced to move out; his father, a deacon of the church sided with him and gave up coming to church. When I went to conduct a communion service there, a pastor of the same name, Li, travelled with me and suggested inviting the estranged deacon to communion and a meal afterwards. Rather reluctantly Pastor Tan agreed, but particularly asked me, in the communion service, to read the Scripture passage about eating and drinking unworthily. The effect was not as I had expected, for during the service Pastor Tan himself rose suddenly and asked the deacon for forgiveness if he had sometimes been too abrupt. Mr Li in turn asked for prayer for himself, and the service concluded amiably with fellowship restored.

The counties of Tehwa and Tatien were subject to sporadic outbursts of banditry. One village was under threat when my Chinese colleague, Mr Sun, and I arrived; at night after the service most villagers went into a large fortified building while the local pastor, Mr Sun and I stayed in the church house. There was no incident that night but we took good care to check the path on the next morning's march. A different kind of hazard was an outbreak of bubonic plague almost every spring and against this we had to be inoculated. The German Jewish doctor working for the Plague Prevention Bureau came to Yungchun periodically for this purpose, and as he enjoyed the hospitality of a western home and food used to stay with me during his visits. A number of Jewish refugees were in China, and the Yungchun Church thoughtfully devoted its 1940 Christmas offering to their relief.

My American colleague, Mrs Jett, was trapped on Kulangsu when the Japanese occupied Amoy in May, 1938. She helped our mission staff there in the splendid work they did among the thousands of refugees who crossed to this island to escape the bombing on the main island. She was able to return to Yungchun in August, but for the next three and a half years attendance at Mission Council meetings on Kulangsu was subject to Japanese passes and a four and a half days journey each way. After Pearl Harbour, December, 1941, all our colleagues in Amoy were put under house-arrest until exchanged with Japanese civilians or transferred to internment camps. Chuanchow then became our main centre. From time to time Japanese air-raids caused damage, including a Church primary school in Tehwa and to one of the churches in Chuanchow. Sometimes the streets were empty as most of the population went out into the country at dawn and did not return till dusk. The Yungchun Chong-Hian School evacuated nearly a thousand feet higher into the hills at So-khi.

I continued my work of visiting the churches, running occasional study groups for pastors and preachers and doing some teaching in the school. We had another visit by a revivalist, Pastor Wang, who encouraged speaking in tongues and was somewhat divisive in relation to the sacraments. Mrs Jett and I met with him to restrain him from extremes; but on the whole the revival meetings encouraged the Church.

By 1944, after nine years, I was long overdue for furlough. The Japanese were intensifying their attempts to link Canton with Hankow by rail which would have completely cut off Fujian from the west. My senior colleague in Chuanchow, Reg Rogers, advised me to leave in the summer while he and the doctors remained. I left Yungchun in June, and with the help of an American airlift from Suichwan to Kweilin, got through to Kunming, India and home.

When I returned to China in spring, 1946, I was stationed in Chuanchow. It was a time of drought and the price of rice soaring. With the fighting up north between nationalists and communists, inflation was a serious problem. In October 1946 I went to Hong Kong to meet my fiancee, Joyce Crichton, and we married in St.John's Cathedral. There was an acute shortage of missionaries, especially ministerial; Boris Anderson and Dan Beeby were still mainly involved in language study. My work continued largely in visiting and encouraging the churches, going down to Unsio and Changpu and as far south as the Guangdong border. With very few motor roads open most travel was by boat or on foot. Back in Chuanchow I kept in touch with the schools, especially Poe-goan (Westminster College), with the flourishing youth groups, and my wife helped with the Women's School. In Chuanchow there were Board meetings for the Schools and Hospital to attend, and in Amoy more meetings, in particular with the representatives of the London Missionary Society and Reformed Church in America. We were engaged in drawing up a plan for transferring property and powers to the Synod, with missionaries coming only at its request and being subject to it regarding placement; in other words, to fulfil the agreement for Self-government of the Chinese Church.

Memories of the last eighteen months are very mixed. Tension was present in the summer of 1949 as the Red Army drew nearer but the city of Chuanchow was taken over peacefully in August though the guns were heard for days as they made their way on to Amoy. The movement of foreigners was restricted unless police permission was first obtained. At times I was able to gather local pastors and preachers in my house but it was not advisable for the pastors to ask me to preach in their churches. However I remember once conducting a service with a government official sitting in the congregation. He was waiting for a meeting with church leaders which was to follow. At the same time, in both schools and churches, youth work flourished, and, having obtained permission, the annual summer conference was held in Chuanchow in 1950. Great emphasis was laid on the spiritual life, and memory preserves their farewell words, "Don't be afraid for us; we shall hold the faith".

Because of the restrictions on mission work and the fear of the Korean War drawing China in officially, Kathleen Duncan, Douglas and Jean Short with their twin babies, and myself, Joyce and our two small children applied in July, 1950, to leave. Eventually our exit permits were granted in November, farewell meetings were held in church and hospital, we made our way to Canton, arrived in Hong Kong on December 14th, and sailed for home on December 22nd.

Ruth (Milne) Oakley *served as a doctor in the Swatow Mission Hospital from 1932 to 1950. She was having medical treatment in Hong Kong in December, 1941, when the Japanese captured the island and was interned in Stanley Camp until the end of the war. After the missionary withdrawal* from China she served in Nigeria with the Church Missionary Society, and then settled in Norfolk on her marriage to Leonard Oakley, a friend from internment days. Extracts of letters written after her release from internment rekindle memories of that time.

Letter dated 3rd September, 1945, from Stanley Camp, Hong Kong

............Life here gets more and more hectic, half the useful people in the camp (or more) have been drafted into Hong Kong to try to straighten things out there a bit, so those who are left are all trying to do other people's jobs as well as their own. About 100 sick people have been taken off on the Hospital ship and I suppose it wont be long before they get the next batch off, then things will get easier. I (being comparatively healthy) will probably have to wait until the end whenever that is. They have managed to get a certain amount of Chinese labour in to help out the Camp, for instance the kitchen in our quarters (one-third of the Camp) was staffed almost entirely by police who got sent into Hong Kong at short notice, leaving the remaining staff very heavy work to do. Preparing food for 700 is no joke. However they have got enough Chinese to help out now I think. The trouble is to find a good O.C. now. All along it has been a difficult job to fill; hard work, lots of kicks and few thanks.

I don't know what to say to you now. There's so much one could say but I don't particularly want to harrow you with all the nasty things that have happened and are now over and done with. I've luckily got the kind of memory that forgets the beastly things and remembers the nice ones. They say there is hope we will get letters tomorrow and that will be a thrill. My last news of you all is March '44 (and 25 words at that.) I'm longing to hear how you all are and news of my friends. This Rip van Winkle feeling is beastly being so out of touch with everything. How one will ever become up-to-date in the medical line I can't imagine. The very thought of three and a half years back numbers of Lancets and BMJs depresses me beyond measure, but perhaps I'll feel more like tackling them later.

I feel in some ways I've rather wasted my time in this Camp in not doing more Chinese study for instance. But I searched the whole Camp (2000) and found no-one who either knew the Swatow dialect or wanted to study it. So I tried working on my own for a bit. Then I found that one of our women Chinese warders came from Swatow and we worked together for a bit; but then the Japanese began beating up the warders for talking to internees and I was afraid of getting her into trouble, so I had to stop that.

If I had known we were going to be here so long I would have set to and learned Cantonese as there were lots of Cantonese classes going; but I was afraid of mixing up my Swatow tones and thought I wouldn't have time to go very far with it, so I didn't. Some people did French or German, Italian or Spanish too; but all along my time seems to have been pretty well occupied. I put a lot of work into the different study-circles and discussion groups I helped to run (at one time I was helping with 6 which meant something nearly every day) and that has all been valuable for me. I have had so little time for real thinking in my 10 years in Swatow that I think it was very good for me to have to consider the intellectual foundations for Christianity afresh. Discussions with agnostics who have lost their faith or never had one make one re-consider the grounds of one's beliefs in the effort to help them find a faith. There have been lots of Canon Streeter's books in the Camp, from St.Stephen's College Library and they have been invaluable in helping people who were trying to think things through, especially "Reality", which has "converted" several people. So many people have never heard of these good books and still think that the Church thinks as she did in the 18th and 19th centuries. So we really have had a chance to clear away some misconceptions and help people to a truer idea of what Christianity really is.....

The medical work I have been able to do has all been out-patient work, and not very taxing from a medical point of view; but good fun from the point of human interest. They have started another Camp at the Catholic Mission, 2 miles from here, for 107 odd people sent there from H.K. and I have been asked to be M.O. thereof. I'm going out every second day for an hour or two and they've also asked me to start a clinic in the village for the Chinese there who have had no medical attention for three and a half years. So those two added to my five camp-clinics and other chores (food-queues, water-queues etc.) keep me fairly busy and help me to forget my impatience and longing to get home. Now there is a chance to get home at last, everyone has become desperately home-sick and longing to see their own folk again. I hope it won't be too long before I see you all again my dearest darlings....."

From the next letter, dated 7th September, 1945, from Stanley Camp

.........I hope you got my two previous letters safely. I've still no news from the outside, except that Dr Moore of the Methodist Mission in Shinkwan (now in the RAMC) has flown in here (from Kunming) and is now taking charge of the medical work in the Camp as so many of the Camp doctors are either invalided home or gone into Hong Kong. Two nice Air Force doctors are also helping him with the clinic etc. I must say I shall be glad to hand over as there's been too much work this last week with the two clinics I'm doing outside the Camp as well. Dr Moore told us the very sad news that a V2 bomb had dropped on our Mission monthly c'ttee six months ago and killed a lot of people.*(On 9th February, 1945, the rocket referred to killed most of the Presbyterian Church's senior officials and other office staff)* As my last news is 15 months old I had heard no word of it and am now awaiting details. I've been so lucky so far in not losing people I love that it's a bit of a shock to realise the possibility of it. I expect I'll hear soon.

Things here remain in great confusion between the Navy and the Civil administration; but two Hospital ships have gone off with the seriously sick and the Empress of Australia is going in another few days with another 2 to 3 thousand so that ought to clear the decks a bit. I may get off on the boat after that with a bit of luck. I understand that they are trying to replace the Govt. servants by other people so as to let them all get a chance to recuperate for some months, but in the meantime they are having a tough time. It is more difficult for the business people who have often no one to take their place. In the meantime the Navy are being so kind, sending things into the Camp, many of them presents from individuals, we keep having to draw lots for the things, tobacco, tooth-paste, shoe-laces etc. Everything is welcome when you are out of everything more or less. A brass band from the Swiftsure came and gave us a concert last night: all Jazz which you know I can't appreciate much: but their obvious goodwill and desire to please us was so touching I thoroughly enjoyed it, even if I am no jazz fan. I find normal people from the outside so interesting. They all seem so beefy and brisk and alert and energetic compared with us. I wonder if I will seem very queer when I get home. If so, please excuse! Our grumbly old lady of 74 is on the next boat to go away, much to our relief. Admittedly there has been plenty to grumble about, but it doesn't help to draw attention to the bad food day after day. Three and a half years of living in the same room has been pretty wearing and I shall say goodbye quite cheerfully. That has been one of the worst things here, the overcrowding. That is why I have spent so much time out of doors, to get away from the old lady's tongue. She has a very kind heart but hides it pretty well. I wonder how long we shall have to wait before we get letters! How I long for news!

We got two apples and an orange each yesterday. What a thrill! I don't know when I tasted anything so good. But the thing I'm really longing for is a hot bath, my last one having been on December 8th, 1941. I can't imagine what layers of dirt will come off me. A cold shower on a concrete floor and inadequate soap made washing a purgatory last winter which was the coldest known in H.K. for 40 years. None of us have ever suffered with the cold as we did last winter, although the temp. only dropped to about 40; but we were getting practically no fats in our diet then and very few people had enough blankets and there was no question of hot-water bottles because the fuel situation was so acute that we were only getting hot water for drinking twice a day instead of three times as we have done through most of the Camp. We really were dreading another winter here and are so thankful to be spared it. I used to walk round and round for about an hour every evening till I got my feet warm before going to bed, which made one beastly hungry; but that was better than lying awake half the night with the cold. We internees should be the most thankful people in the world after this. Everything will seem so good to us !

I can't discuss family news till I hear from you. So I hope I hear soon!......

After distinguished service as a pilot in the Royal Flying Corps during the First World War, **Robert Tully**, *a science graduate of Glasgow University, went out to teach in the Amoy Anglo-Chinese College in 1922. Twenty years later he and his family were interned by the Japanese in a Shanghai camp for three and a half years. He and Mrs Tully returned to Amoy in 1946 and as senior missionary he carried the main burden of responsibility from then to the final withdrawal in 1951. From 1952 he gave valuable service in the development of the Presbyterian Boys School in Singapore. He died only a few weeks after returning home on retirement in 1963. The two letters which follow, written to Bill Short, formerly a South Fujian missionary colleague, but then Foreign Missions Secretary in London, describe conditions in Kulangsu, Amoy, before the final withdrawal of the Nationalist forces from the mainland.*

"Amoy, 11th October, 1949
.........For the present the Amoy Local Committee must act independently of Chuanchow (Qanzhou) as for the past six weeks there have been no communications with that centre. (*Chuanchow had been liberated on August 31st*) The last letter was dated 31st August and since then no news from any

source regarding the welfare of that city. For the past three to four weeks Amoy and Kulangsu have been completely cut off from the mainland and there are no communications possible as the whole island is an armed camp with soldiers and defence works everywhere. On account of its relationship to the mainland Kulangsu so far has come in for the largest share of the activities and we seldom have long periods free from gunfire. One day last week a shell (aerial torpedo) struck the roof of our house making a big hole through roof and ceiling just above the head of the stairway. Fortunately no one was injured by that shell (apart from minor scratches to a teacher crossing the playground), but Mrs Tully was on the verandah at the time, a few yards away, and I had just come in from school and was pouring myself a cup of tea. About the same time a second shell landed in the school grounds and another hit buildings near the bank house. We speedily moved to the two rooms downstairs and are eating in the hallway. Lai-chu-oh has had a lot of destruction and many people have moved out. The two houses next to ours have been evacuated. It was fortunate that it did not take place on the previous day when we had a typhoon and under these circumstances not much of the roof might have remained. However I have been able to get the roof repaired to prevent further deterioration. Kathlyn says she will move after we have been hit three times but I am standing out for seven! One consolation is that the soldiers no longer want to take up residence with us!

On the following night we had a tremendous amount of shelling going on from the government side and I thought there was a real attack taking place. As you have guns to right of you, guns to left of you and guns behind you (firing from Amoy positions) it makes a lot of noise, and according to the official report seven thousand shells were fired that night. Now all this might sound quite exciting but it is mostly sound and fury. The important thing is that I cant see how either side is to achieve success and it looks as if this state of affairs may go on for months with a steady deterioration of the situation. Even now you cannot buy meat or eggs and the cost of everything is prohibitive. For the past six weeks there have been no sea products of any kind as all sea junks were seized and no sampans are allowed. As so many are unemployed and shops do no business the economic situation must get worse and worse. Then with so many thousands of soldiers and people leaving certain areas and crowding into others the whole place is rapidly becoming a universal latrine without sanitary conditions so that helped by undernourishment there may be all sorts of epidemics. I think I have said enough to show that this really is no place for small children and it is better that they should take the opportunity of getting out with the 'Anhui' which will probably be the last boat for an indefinite period.

........I am afraid this letter is somewhat disjointed as I have been called away and interrupted almost constantly with urgent problems and the difficulties which constantly arise. For example at midday I got word that gun emplacements were being dug in the Missionary Cemetery and hastened down to Lai-chu-oh to find that the emplacement had involved digging into four of the graves although the coffins did not appear to have been disturbed. Actually they were all those of children including a child of Poppen and one of De Pree's *(American Reformed Church missionaries)*. I went to see the Consul about it but as Chinese graves are being opened all over the place it is difficult to see what can be done about it.

.......The war and all that I have mentioned above is really a minor part of our troubles. It is inadvisable to put much on paper but Beeby will tell you about things. I have had really a terribly difficult time through the activities of the Military Political Police. One night three weeks ago they came to arrest five members of the staff including the principal, his wife, the dean of studies and two others. Of these Kho effected his escape but the other four were taken off although none of them had been active politically. Since then naturally no one will take any responsibility and I have to be everything, take all decisions and hold everything together. I have had an exceedingly difficult time trying to negotiate for their release and even the getting to and fro to Amoy was no easy matter. Everyone is scared and I have had great difficulty in keeping others from going into hiding which is no easy matter with registrations, mutual guarantees, house-searching, arrests etc. and of course it is impossible to get off the islands.......With the arrests etc. we were running with seven teachers short and it has been a business keeping things going; but I fear if I were not constantly about things would soon fall to pieces. Actually it is wonderful how we have got on. Today I have had word that we can get the release of Mrs Kho on the guarantee of three shops and hope that it may be possible to get this fixed up tomorrow.......If I have said too much about troubles don't take them too seriously. Other people's are much worse and there is a funny side to most things. It is good of Yule to remain. Please thank his Church. Both the ladies (*i.e.WMA staff*) are well and in excellent spirits. I have not heard of the boxes I sent to Vardons *(Travel agents)*. Did they arrive all right? Greetings to all

                                    Yours sincerely,   Robert Tully

Three days later, 14th October, after describing the perpetual noise of firing which had been going on for four weeks, Tully wrote,
"It is the thousand and one other things that have to be attended to that take the most out of one and with the poor feeding one gets terribly tired. When the Japs were here you could get the cheaper sea foods and we had hens and a goat, but now there is but little that one can afford and of course an egg at half -a -crown is out of the question. There is a lot of tinned things still in the shops but the prices are completely prohibitive. If only one had more energy! Actually there have not been very many casualties so far and in many ways things go on as usual. Two nights ago our dog whined to get into the bedroom and then produced four pups! The school continues with about 600 students but requires constant nursing to keep the wheels turning as no one will dare to take any responsibility so that I have to be the authority for everything.

I understand that Canton is to be handed over tomorrow and wonder if it will affect things here. As I write there is a tremendous lot of shell and machine gun fire going on mostly in the direction of Lam Tai Bu and the harbour entrance. I hope it will still be possible for boats to get in and out from time to time. If this is to go on for months we will all be needing relief by next year! A silver dollar is equal to about five shillings and seems to go nowhere. Probably our greatest difficulties will continue to be economic and everything is so expensive. Grants when converted into silver seem so little to the recipients that they do not realize how much it is in sterling to those at home."

And then a P.S. "Early Sat. morning (15th). The Anhui is signalled to come in so must hand this over to Beeby. We are all well and send greetings to all at home. Kindest regards. Yours very sincerely

RobertTully"

After training at Carey Hall, **Margaret Wright** *went to Swatow as a WMA missionary in 1936.* **Tony Strange** *arrived in 1937 to serve as a doctor in the Swatow Mission Hospital. They were married in 1938. War time conditions both inside and outside China caused them and their family long periods of separation. The same conditions also produced an abundance of family letters, from one of which the following is an extract.*

"4th December 1949

Our "liberation" took place on 24th October, and it was most welcome after the uncertainty of the previous four days. The main body of Nationalist soldiers left on 20th October, which was a day of great activity. Martial law was in force until afternoon, with the result that we had practically no out-patients. During the morning there were several explosions which were an attempt to make the aerodrome useless, but no great damage was done. Our greatest concern was lest the water and electricity plants should be blown up, but it is said that the two companies paid the necessary amount of "squeeze" to the departing military, and so avoided that fate. However apparently the Telephone Co. did not come up to scratch, and the exchange was so damaged as to be put out of action. The soldiers mostly left in transports that afternoon, but some small naval vessels remained and that night sailors came ashore and did some looting and shooting. In Swatow there are various Buddhist Charitable Guilds which do a bit of relief work, and they organised numerous bodies of people armed with lights and wooden poles who patrolled the streets in an effort to stop looting. Some living in very many of the little narrow streets joined together to erect big wooden gates at each end of the street, to prevent looters getting in.

We were a bit apprehensive that the soldiers leaving their quarters next to the Hospital might set them on fire, as happened before the Japanese arrived in 1939, but this was not done, and late in the afternoon some more soldiers arrived whose loyalty to the Nationalist Govt. does not seem to have been very great, and they took up their quarters there. They helped to keep order until the Communists arrived. On the night of the 21st there was an effort by armed people in from the country to enter Swatow, presumably to loot, but this was repulsed. We had expected looting from the army, but not from the navy, whose traditions we thought would inspire a higher level of conduct.

After these nights everything was quiet until the Communists arrived. On 23rd October the "liberation" flag was hoisted on the building next to the Hospital, and on the following afternoon the troops arrived in their blue uniforms.

There was some confusion in the couple of weeks before the Nationalist troops left. The Press Gangs were presumably trying to make up their number before going to Formosa, and they were working not only in Swatow but in the country districts around as well. The result of the loss of family breadwinners can be imagined. Also during these last few weeks heavy extra taxes were levied on all imports and exports by the military, who collected the proceeds, while wealthy business men had big demands levied on them with the result that they were forced to go to Hong Kong. The Army commanders milked the city well before their unlamented departure.

After the day of liberation people were very apprehensive of air-raids from Formosa, but there was only one small one three weeks ago on a small British ship that came into the harbour. There were a small number of casualties, of whom we admitted five, We have had quite a number of "liberation" soldiers as patients. They have been well-behaved, easy to manage, and appreciative of the treatment they receive, and have paid for most of it. Some of them have been referred to us from other hospitals and we are hoping for a friendly relationship with them - one being a military hospital, and the other the Government civilian hospital. We received payment for three of the air-raid casualties we had already discharged, although we said we were prepared to treat them like any other patients, who only pay if they have the means to do so.

On the day of liberation fourteen of our student nurses left without notice to join the Liberation Health Corps, to which they had already had written invitations. They were almost equally divided between the first three years, and there has been much unsettlement amongst those who remained. Some of those who have left have taken the line that those who served in Mission Hospitals were puppets, as missionary doctors were agents of foreign governments; previously they were perfectly friendly with us. We hope that those who remain will realise that they can serve their country in a Mission hospital, and that missionaries also welcome the liberation, after the previous corrupt regime. There has been great enthusiasm for the liberation, particularly among young folk in their teens, and it has captured their imagination, and made them feel that they have a real share in their country. There has been, not unnaturally, a ready assumption that those older than themselves belong to the past, and are therefore reactionary - that they need their minds washed, a common expression. These young folk place great emphasis on the freedom that has been achieved, and so discipline has not been easy, but the Liberation Army is well disciplined.

The departure of these student nurses made things difficult for us and we had to close down beds, reducing our total from 130 to 107, which is the number we had a year ago. The situation would have been still more difficult had not the new class of probationers taken in last September just finished their preliminary lectures and been ready to start in the wards. We were so pleased at having reached our figure of 130 beds, which was the number we planned to have, and now we have to climb up the hill again. May there be no worse things in store for us!

After shipping ceased coming from Hong Kong prices of all foreign goods, particularly medicines, soared. However, boats are now running at regular, if not very frequent, intervals, and prices have come down, and this Government is allowing most medicines in duty free. We had already laid in good stocks of most drugs.

Last weekend we had three days of celebrations for the Liberation, and on Friday night there was a grand torchlight procession which took three hours to pass. We had a good view of it from our upstairs verandah, and our nurses took part in it. John and Anne *(their children)* were absolutely thrilled. The last time I watched a procession was when the Japanese organised one in February, 1942, to celebrate the fall of Singapore!

We hope it will not be long before the British Government recognises China's new government; the area it controls seems to merit recognition. We are also looking forward to the day when ships are running regularly between here and Hong Kong. The rice harvest is good and rice is now cheap."

After some years in the world of insurance, **Jim Waddell** *trained for the ministry and offered for missionary service. He and Mrs Waddell served in Swatow and Swabue from 1932 onwards. During the Japanese occupation Jim was based in Wukingfu but returned to Swabue after the war ended. He was on furlough when Swabue was liberated and the letter below describes the circumstances of his return and first impressions. After the missionary withdrawal he served for four years in Malaya as an Emergency Administration Officer, working among Chaozhou speaking New Villages, and then resumed his missionary service in the Malaya Synod of the Chinese Christian Church. His final period of overseas service was alongside his former colleague in Swabue, Dr Neil Fraser, in the Leprosy Mission in Hong Kong at Hay-ling-chau, the Isle of Happy Healing.*

Letter from Swabue, dated 28th November, 1949, to the O.M. Secretary, F.G.Healey
Dear Healey,
    After my wait of five weeks in Hong Kong unable to secure a passage, and after several false alarms, I eventually managed to get here yesterday on a boat in which Dr Zi's family has an interest*(Dr Zi was formerly principal of the Swatow Pue-li Theological College)*. The boat is a motor vessel of over 200 tons, built in U.S.A. in 1943, recently acquired by a Chinese Company in Hong Kong, and put onto the Swabue blockade-running. It does not officially carry passengers, but I was given a free trip, and having "borrowed" a bunk from one of the crew, had a fairly smooth trip. We left about nine in the evening, and were in sight of Swabue soon after dawn, when we bumped on to a sandbank. About three-quarters of an hour of maneuvering got us free, and we proceeded into harbour. After casting anchor, we were immediately boarded by a party of soldiers, mostly youngsters, some with rifles and some with pistols on both hips. A few of them fired off wild shots out of sheer joie-de-vivre! The former Customs service has ceased, and some of the soldiers who belonged to a group called "Army Customs Society" searched the ship and examined the baggage in great detail. Mine was only given a very perfunctory examination. I declared some medicines and groceries, but explained they were for Hospital and personal use. After discussion they sent a soldier off with me to take me to the Customs office, where in spite of a milling crowd, he got hold of an official who promptly came over and gave my goods free entry.

    Soldiers and officials were all local men, (which makes life much easier than when one has to persuade Northerners or Cantonese who speak incomprehensible languages), and they were all extremely affable and helpful. The fact that I was expected had been duly notified, and no exception taken to my re-entry. I didn't even have to show my passport and visa. It was all quite casual and friendly. Some of the new officials are, I gather, ex-pupils of the Mission School. This may be a temporary phase, and there may be a new line up of officialdom at no distant date, but meanwhile it is pleasant to have local people, and entry has been simplified. There are various people in Hong Kong, some who have been waiting many months and others who came out with me on the "Carthage", who want to get in by the more significant ports, but they can't get in without permits, and their applications are producing no results.

    Miss Paton is back here from Swatow, having travelled overland. She and Miss Downward were at Church when I arrived. Fraser met me just outside the Compound. He had heard I was on the boat, and had gone out in our sampan to meet me, but I had already gone off to the Customs. Church, Hospital and School are all proceeding on a more or less normal course, though there are certain undercurrents and divisive tendencies apparent, due not to political interference but to lack of Christian stability, particularly among the younger elements, who perhaps more than their seniors are excited by the revolutionary spirit of the times I'll see gradually how things are trending, but meanwhile the work goes on, with encouragement in some directions from the new authorities. This is just a preliminary note to tell of my arrival. More news will follow.

  Kindest regards,
Yours very sincerely
Jas Waddell

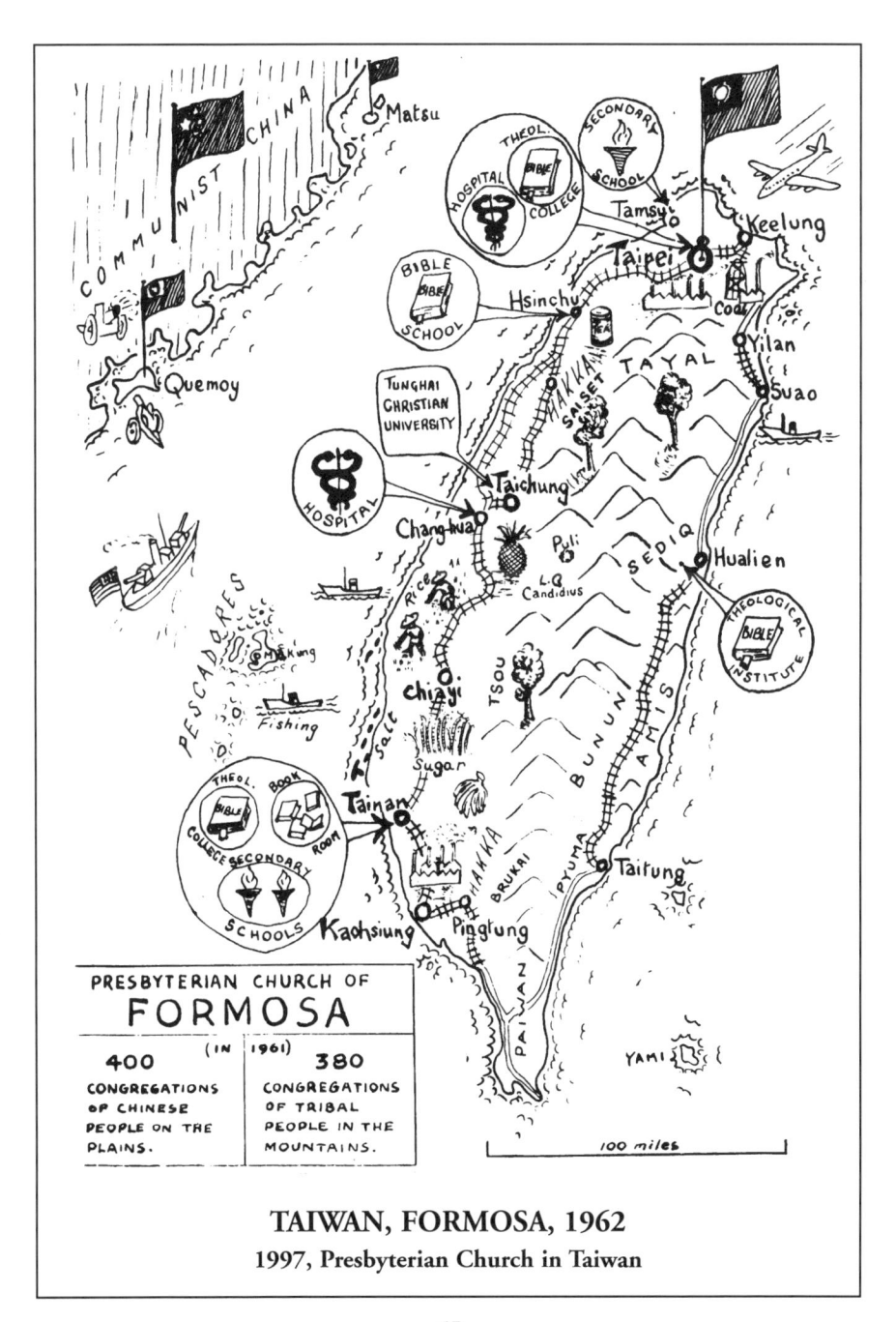

Pilgrims in Mission   *Memories: Taiwan*

TAIWAN, FORMOSA, 1962
1997, Presbyterian Church in Taiwan

MEMORIES: TAIWAN

Boris and Clare Anderson *served in Chuanchow, South Fujian from 1946 to 1948 and were then transferred to Tainan, Taiwan, serving there till 1963. At the end of 1964 Boris took up the work of OM Secretary to which he had been appointed the previous year. From 1972 he served the United Reformed Church as Secretary of the World Church and Mission Department until retirement in 1983.*

When a telegram suddenly arrived from London in the summer of 1948, telling us we had been re-appointed from South Fukien to Taiwan, we were taken aback. We had only had two years in China and were just beginning to get the hang of things (including the language); and had made many friends we would now have to leave. But when we got to Taiwan we soon found ourselves caught up in the new situation.

The Presbyterian Church there, virtually the only Protestant church in the island at that time, was just beginning to find its feet again after 15 years of Japanese military domination and from the stigma and oppression which arose from its close association with British (and therefore enemy) missionaries, and, as the army saw it, with Western values and thought systems. During those long, painful years the church had endured much hardship; and there had been one or two failures. There had been much heart-searching too on such tangled questions as respective loyalties to the Emperor and to Jesus Christ. But on the whole the small Christian community had successfully survived both the police crackdown and the absence of missionaries and mission funds. Though physically somewhat run-down, it was spiritually wide awake and confident in itself and in its Lord. As far as the Southern Synod was concerned (to which the English Presbyterians were attached), there was an immensely open and united attitude and an eagerness for advance. Theologically and socially it was a really solid church. All it needed was imaginative leadership.

It was soon clear to us that the leadership was there. I could easily mention thirty or forty really outstanding people, but must confine myself to two. It is not too much to say that between them, and of course with the back-up they had from very many others, they transformed the church. The years 1948-1965 were not only a time of consolidation and expansion in Taiwan, but a time when, as one of the two said, the Presbyterian Church of Taiwan entered the world stage.

The first of these two was Shoki Coe, son of a pastor, who had had his higher education in Tokyo and Cambridge, married an English wife, been active especially in church youth groups in England, and had arrived back in Taiwan a year before Clare and I got there. The church appointed him to be the first Taiwanese Principal of Tainan Theological College, just re-opened after eight years closure through Japanese pressure. There was everything for him to do - buildings to be restored and extended, library to be restocked, study courses to be worked out and suitable students to be sought. I had got to know Shoki in England and he was (he died in 1988) the closest friend I ever had. Both Clare and I taught in the college - in fact the church was generous enough to appoint me Vice-Principal - and many and long were the discussions we had together and with others about how to train a worthy ministry for the church. In the early 1950s Shoki and the college attracted the attention of a number of American church leaders, and with their backing, the college was able to expand from 17 students when we arrived to over 200 well before we left.

Shoki was also much taken up with university students and other young people generally, and played a big part in founding an immensely active youth organisation.

But there were two other matters even more central to the life of the church - its unity and its outreach. Though on paper the Presbyterian Church in Taiwan was a unity, the north and south churches, with their different supporting missions, were effectively two churches. The problem was to persuade the northern church to integrate with the south. For one thing, the Canadian 'mission field' in the north had at the formation of the United Church of Canada in the 1920s been allocated, in spite of missionary protest, to the minority 'continuing Presbyterians', who had refused to unite with Canadian Congregationalists and Methodists. There was therefore inevitability a kind of 'anti-union' ethos in the north of Taiwan. For another thing, the northern church was only about a third the size of its southern sister, so many of the members, understandably, feared being 'swallowed' by the south and outvoted on every issue in a united church.

And here I must introduce the second man who to my mind, with Shoki, made all the difference to the ultimate success of the union (and the church's outreach). He was Ng-Butong, a man with much less international experience than Shoki, but with a much deeper and more detailed knowledge of Taiwanese life and culture - and of church politics! He was a wonderful orator in Taiwanese, powerful and moving, and was a sound administrator. He had already been chosen as the first full-time General Secretary of the Southern Synod, and as such was at the forefront of negotiations with the north, which after long years of effort finally came to fruition.

Bu-tong was equally involved in the church's outreach, both before and after the union, when he became General Secretary of the whole church. A long debate in the Synod of 1954 concluded that to reach all Taiwanese effectively, there needed to be a church within walking distance (say 3 miles) of the bulk of the population; and that to achieve this, twice as many churches as the Synod then had would be needed. It was unanimously decided to make this the goal of the church's centenary celebrations in 1965. So began the ten year 'Double the Churches' movement. This, I believe, could not have succeeded, as it did, without Bu-tong at the centre and around in towns and villages - observing, planning and co-ordinating the work of thousands of others.

After the centenary, the Shoki - Bu-tong partnership (or 'Hwang Dynasty' as it was irreverently called: the two men sharing the same surname, read as Hwang in mandarin Chinese) broke up as the two left to work with international church organisations. Another generation took over. But from abroad (one in England and one in the USA) these two did play a great part in the next item on the church's agenda - the democratisation of Taiwan. But that is another story. And by this time Clare and I had left Taiwan too. Jane and Robin needed more advanced education than we could provide in Tainan, and anyway there were young, well-trained Taiwanese ready and keen to take on our teaching schedules. So though it was hard to leave so much of our lives behind, we have never thought we made the wrong decision.

***Dan and Joyce Beeby** served in Amoy, South Fujian, from 1946 to 1949 and were then transferred to Taiwan. In 1972 they were deported by the Kuomintang administration and returned to the UK. Dan served in the Selly Oak Colleges as O.T.Lecturer from 1972 till his retirement in 1986, and during the last five years of that period was also Principal of St. Andrew's Hall. The following extract, quoted by permission, is from an article Dan wrote in 1993 on My Pilgrimage in Mission for the International Bulletin of Missionary Research*

To begin at the very beginning there was the mother who doted on me, even though it meant leaving her for five years at a time. There was the father who never seemed to understand and provided a model for me to react against. There was the sister who stayed that I might go. There was the Anglican fiancee who resisted parental pressure and married a Presbyterian pacifist to go with him to China. There was the wild fundamentalist preacher who set fire to my even wilder liberalism; the professor of philosophy, recommended for the Victoria Cross in the First World War, who cared for, tolerated, guided and inspired the callow but committed pacifist in the Second World War; the Chinese and Taiwanese brother and sister ministers, sacrificial and loving, who cared for us and still care; the students, many of whom have surpassed their teachers, who put me right, taught me the real language (including the swear words), who loved me enough to put me and keep on putting me right. There was Jim Muilenburg, who nursed me through a doctorate at Union Theological Seminary, New York City. And then there was Shoki (alias Shoki Ko, Dr. Coe, the Rev. C.H.Hwang, Ng Chiong Hui, et al.) church leader extraordinary who was friend, mentor, boss, and pastor and without whom the journey would have been unthinkable.

There were the names I knew through countless books. Constant companions were the bridge builders: C.S.Lewis who bridged the gap between poet and preacher; Karl Barth, who brought together the words of men and the Word of God; Jim Muilenburg, linking rhetoric and theology; and John Donne, who married the sensuous and the sacred.

Today the pilgrim party is still growing, in China, Taiwan, worldwide; and at home, as our children still try to educate me, and my grandchildren rub my nose in the exciting reality of the present.

Learning on the Way

After twenty years' exile I was recently allowed a short visit to Taiwan. I went knowing that great changes had taken place and that I had to learn about the new Taiwan. I also knew that the Dan Beeby being welcomed by the church was not the one I knew. I had to learn who the "new me" was. So I went to learn. For someone being welcomed as an old teacher, I assumed that the learning role had to be learned but I found that it came rather easily because the attempt to learn triggered the realization that my role had always been a learning role. I had taught and communicated, instructed, changed minds, and "converted" (more anon), but I discovered that the giving in no way matched the learning and receiving.

In learning their language, I had learned more of my own. In learning to be Taiwanese, I understood what it was to be English. In learning their culture, I learned that I also had a culture and that in forming me, it had at the same time distorted me. I learned that there were strong links between culture and preaching and that cultures, particularly my culture, could blind one to the Christ I preached. I learned to hear the unsaid in another culture, to see new glimpses of new unsuspected beauties. I discovered that the unthinkable was regularly thought by some people and that laughter outside Europe had surprising overtones and depths. Then there was the new viewpoint that first shattered and then began to refashion one, and there was the patience and tolerance and love of colleagues with one in the refashioning. There was the slow realization that God was an Asian man who went to Africa but never Europe, that the Word of God was almost all Asian, and that early theology was mostly African and that most of "my Europe" was the gift of people from Jerusalem and Alexandria and Nicaea and Carthage.

The Greatest Lesson

In 1972, soon after the Presbyterian Church of Taiwan published the first of its statements on the political situation in Taiwan - perhaps the first ever such statement made by a church of Chinese race - I was expelled. The events leading up to the statement and my expulsion will always be linked to Tainan Theological College's lectionary readings of Exodus in the autumn of 1971. Daily as we read and preached, Taiwan became Israel in Egypt. Sometimes we were Moses and strong, sometimes we murmured in fear with Israel, and sometimes we saw that even Pharaoh had a point. I knew absolutely that we had to follow Moses and follow the hazardous path of claiming liberty. At the same time I was not allowed to forget the exile and its opposite teaching. God never opened my ear to hear "set my people free," but he also told me to read Jeremiah 29. At age fifty, this professor of Old Testament began his education all over again. On the field of politics, classroom hermeneutics became a matter of life and death.

I now see the worst time of my life was also the best. Miserable at being exiled, we rejoiced at the spontaneous, almost unbelievable demonstrations of love and concern from the church in Taiwan, which have never ceased. Indeed despite twenty years absence, they have grown. It was worst and best because although banished and deprived, my reading of Scripture began afresh in that dialogue between Exodus and Jeremiah. Twenty-five years of teaching culminated in my hardest lesson and a new beginning in thought and ministry. There came new understandings of the cross and "Good Friday", a new understanding of the strength of vulnerability, of the truth in contradiction, of why, in knowing "only one thing" one inherits the earth.

The Unseen Hand

As I move from the pilgrimage problem to the final question, is it possible to see any design? Has it been yet another ramble of yet another "rolling English drunkard," or do some patterns emerge?

We volunteered for India but went protestingly to China. Ejected from China, we went reluctantly to Taiwan. Once, absent in the United States, I returned to Taiwan to find myself (very unwillingly) appointed a professor of Old Testament. Ten years later my plans to spend a year in Israel were frustrated by Shoki's insistence that I should go to Union Theological Seminary, New York, to take a doctorate. Jim Muilenburg supported him, so I went. In 1972 I became an exile from Taiwan, reluctantly returned to England, and, rather ungraciously, stayed there instead of accepting offers in the Far East. At sixty-six I retired reluctantly, and I am sure that before long I shall die protestingly. A tale of reluctance and perhaps of rebellion, but that is only my contribution to the journey and it (thank God) is not the whole story. Reflecting at leisure, I have to admit (somewhat reluctantly) that every time I was overruled and pushed protesting to what I did not want to do, I later found myself in a large place and my path strewn with blessings. Through a glass darkly a pattern emerges; it is the pattern of resistance, gracious overruling, and a blessing only later acknowledged.

The pattern is not a new one. It is the movement from dark to light, night to day. It was this pattern in 1972 when our worst day became our best day. It is the pattern of bondage and exodus, sin and forgiveness, descent and ascent, crucifixion and resurrection. It is the language of the Bible; it is perhaps the central and ubiquitous theme of the whole of Scripture, and it is pilgrimage language. Has the ramble been a pilgrimage after all?

Kathleen Moody served in Taiwan from 1948 till her retirement in 1985. Initially appointed for social work she found her ministry increasingly in music, in the Tainan Theological College and throughout the church.

I went to Taiwan in November 1948. After five months I took my first language exam, written and spoken. The latter was taken by a Taiwanese teacher who was Matron in our Girls' School and had known several generations of people from overseas. One of the questions she asked me was "How many 'Soan-kau-su' (missionaries) do you know?" and to her surprise I answered cheerfully 'I don't know any'. In somewhat shocked tones she said 'But you are one'. This was duly reported to Dr. Shoki Coe who was overseeing all my exams and his response was to laugh and say 'Good! the fact that you did not know the word for "missionary" means that you are learning to belong to the church and to the people of Taiwan and you do not think of yourself as a member of a Mission'.

This was true of all my life in Taiwan. I was welcomed, given affection and friendship, help and support, and always assured that I did indeed 'belong'. In fact, not long after my arrival in the island, there was an Old Students' Re-union at the Girls' School. As the newest recruit I was introduced to the various officers of the Alumni Association, women of influence in the church, many of whom had been among the first girls to receive education and who valued that - gifted, able people who led full and busy lives. When I met Mrs. T.G.Lee, the President, she said to me 'Since I first heard that you were coming to Taiwan I have prayed for you every day. I still do'. This astonished me then and it still does that an older woman in her position with responsibilities in her family, in the church and in many other areas, still found time to pray daily for an unknown, untried young woman coming from another country. I valued what she said and I have never forgotten her words.

As soon as I arrived I was asked to teach the choir in our local East Gate Church - a big congregation and the church where students from both our Boys' and Girls' Schools attended each Sunday. The choir, all young people from the church and the schools, were eager and willing to learn. I was happy to teach but at that time I had only a very few words of Taiwanese. But every Thursday evening the minister of the Church, the Rev. N.S.Niu came to the choir practice, not to take over but to be there if I needed him. It must have taken time from his already crowded days - and nights - but he did it and in so doing helped me to fit in, to learn and to grow in experience and understanding.

Before long Dr Coe who was then Principal of Tainan Theological College asked me to take on teaching music, first to the theology students and then to those in the Kindergarten and Social Work Departments, and later in the newly-established music department. So I had the privilege for thirty-seven years of training future ministers of the church, a vital task in a church known all over Asia as 'The Singing Church'. Graduates of the college serve all over Taiwan and also overseas and, of them, one is now known world-wide for his work in church music - Dr. I-to Loh. He comes from a family which is highly talented musically so, although he came as a theological student, he took all the available music courses and distinguished himself, finally winning the prize for his thesis on 'The History of Hymnody' - his title for that was 'Praise from Jerusalem to Taiwan'. When he graduated he was invited to stay on as Assistant in the Music Department and then went to America to gain his Master's Degree, before returning to join the college Faculty. I was head of the music department then and, after one year, I asked that he and I should change places and that he should be in charge of all the music training in the college while I remained a teacher. It was a happy and fulfilling experience and again one which I valued deeply. Later he returned to America to obtain his doctorate in Ethno-Musicology. He has now returned to Taiwan and is Principal of the college bringing to his task all his gifts, his training, his experience and his commitment. It was a joy to work with him, and to share, under his direction, in strengthening and developing music and worship in the college and the church. There was just one 'problem' - Dr Loh is a composer and the music he has written is very typically his own - modern yet deeply rooted in Taiwan, interesting to study and to sing, but by no means easy. And so the times when I had to conduct one of his own works, as at his ordination, in his presence did not make for relaxed calm. Though I usually found the experience exciting.

But what of my experience as a member of the Presbyterian Church of England? My membership was very important to me. The P.C. of E. was a small church and so every missionary was really known individually, where we served and the work we did was familiar to the church here in England, and when we came on leave we came to a church of which we were truly a part. The overseas work was under the Overseas Mission Committee with a vital and integral place at the centre of the work of the church. And so, one summer, while in this country, I was asked to second the report of that Committee during the General Assembly and I was given complete freedom to say exactly what I wanted to say. This reminded me of my responsibilities to the church here, but it also gave me the opportunity to express to the members of the General Assembly what I felt and believed about the work overseas in which we all shared.

As I look back, re-read what I have remembered and written, I give thanks for the great heritage into which I came. The early missionaries in Taiwan had founded a church. They established a theological college, schools and hospitals with one very clear aim - to show forth Christ, to tell the good news, and in so doing to help into being a strong, independent church. The Presbyterian Church in Taiwan has deep affection for and appreciation of the church here. It is a church which now welcomes fellow-workers from countries around the world, a church which has been tested and has stood firm, a church which has an honoured place in the world-wide church. That this is so is the gift which the Presbyterian Church of England gave to its brothers and sisters in Taiwan.

David Landsborough *served in the Chuanchow Hospital, South Fujian, from 1940 to 1946, and then with his wife **Jean**, also a doctor, from 1947 to 1951. After the missionary withdrawal they were re-appointed to Changhua, Taiwan, where David was born and brought up, and served there till retirement in 1980.*

My 'missionary' memories cover the whole of my life. As a small boy I grew up in a market town, Changhua in central Taiwan. My parents were fully occupied in their work as missionaries; my father in the mission hospital he had founded there, my mother as Sunday School superintendent in the church in the middle of the town where I was a barefooted scholar like the other children and learnt to read the romanised Chinese Bible and hymnbook. My mother also worked with the women of the church and visited the families in and outside the town. She started a choir for the young people of the church, and introduced part-singing. This stimulated interest in western music, and with other churches doing the same, influenced hymn-singing throughout the island. I watched my saintly father as he did his rounds with his "students", in those days in the hospital, and observed him seeing patients in their homes.

Every few months my father would take the train to Tainan in the south for "Council"; there was almost a hush at the mention of the Mission Council. It was evidently very important.

My mother taught me at home from the age of five to eight. During furlough, with some painful adjustment, I was able to fit into English school life. But because some of the boys were convinced I was Chinese, my nickname was obvious. Back in Taiwan again, from the age of eleven to sixteen, I was sent to a spartan boarding-school in Chefoo, North China. Once a year my sister and I returned to Taiwan, for five weeks every Christmas, long enough for us to pick up our much-loved Taiwanese language again, enjoy the warmth and the food, and renew childhood and teenage friendships.

Undoubtedly, I was influenced by what I saw of the work of

missionaries, my parents and others, to decide to be a Christian doctor within the framework of the missionary movement.

In April, 1940, when Norman Tunnell and I arrived in Chuanchow (Quanzhou) as new doctors for the E.P.Mission Hospital there, the Sino-Japanese war had been going on for three years. Although Amoy was in Japanesse hands and Chuanchow suffered from their air-raids, the city was never occupied, and the hospital remained open throughout. We were kept at full stretch all the time. As a brash new recruit I owed much to my colleagues, in and outside the hospital, both Chinese and missionary, and learnt much from them, for I made many mistakes. In the midst of war, plague, deprivation, and sky-rocketing inflation I was impressed by the faith and calm of Chinese Christians.

Two memories of that time come to mind. In our isolation wards there were always patients with typhoid fever. It was before chloramphenicol, the first effective anti-biotic for typhoid, was known. Patients would run their course of three to four weeks of high fever, the second week being the most dangerous period.

There was a farmer beginning his second week. Once he said to me in the midst of his fever, "When you come in to see me, it makes me glad". He seemed to be holding his own, so one night, being very tired, I did not go to see him, thinking, "he's probably all right".

Next morning I did the ward-round and came to his cubicle - an empty bed. I still remember the appalling sense of loss and guilt.

During the war there were three successive years of spring-time bubonic plague. One day a girl was brought in semi-conscious, with a high fever and a bubo (acute swelling of a lymphnode in the groin). For diagnosis we would put a needle into the bubo, withdraw a speck of fluid, and under the microscope confirm the presence of plague bacilli. In this case I unwisely did not wait for a nurse to come and help, but put the needle in. The patient jumped a little, the needle came out of the bubo and grazed one of my fingers with its tip. The patient was admitted to hospital.

I went to see Norman Tunnell with the question, "What do you advise?" He had a diploma in tropical medicine so I could not have done better. He anaesthetised my finger, cut out a small wedge of skin which included completely the graze (and the bacilli if they were there). I remained well. I am sure he saved my life.

Sadly the girl died within 24 hours.

Memories of returning to Chuanchow after the war, in 1947, are of an expanding Chinese hospital. With my wife Jean, Douglas and Jean Short, all three of them doctors, and with Norman's wife, Phyllis, giving extra help to Dorothy Keningale in the nursing, its service to the community was strengthened. A Board of Trustees was formed, consisting of church leaders and helpful representatives of society. But from the end of August, 1949, when the city and surrounding district came under the new government's control, and over the next eighteen months, there were increasing restrictions and growing antagonism to the foreign presence. Phyllis and Norman Tunnell, Jean and I were the last to leave Chuanchow, in early 1951. To leave our colleagues and friends with whom we had worked through the war was a painful experience and a sad memory.

By contrast, our return in 1952 to live in Taiwan was very exciting. Jean also had Taiwan missionary connections for her aunt, Sabine Mackintosh, had taught for many years in the Girls' School in Tainan. For me, to worship again in the church I had attended as a boy, and joined when I was fourteen, was moving. But things were different. The Taiwanese Church had passed through years of hardship. We were now there, not by any mission body authority, but as their guests, invited to come and help in the service of God.

When we arrived the old hospital building, built about 1908, was still standing and in use. But a new superintendent, with a new staff had been appointed and were already at work. I was pleased to walk the wards where my father had worked. In the beautiful countryside of mountains and coast, as yet unspoilt by new buildings, our family enjoyed life there in the same way as I had done as a boy.

Between 1952 and 1980, when we retired, the hospital grew, the scope of its service widened, and it was entirely rebuilt. This was achieved through the wise guidance of a church-appointed Board of Trustees, and the support, both financial and in personnel from Presbyterian Churches in Taiwan, England, the USA and Canada, and significant grants from other sources such as the gift of a large sum for the rebuilding from the Methodist Church, USA. The foundation stone of the first stage of rebuilding bore the words, 'For no one can lay any foundation than that already laid which is Jesus Christ', and the logo we chose for the hospital was a single-line drawing of Jesus washing his disciples' feet.

The genuine and firm faith of fellow-Christians helped me and confirmed my own faith. Both in Chuanchow and Changhua. Jean and I felt we were utterly dependent on our Chinese colleagues. The worth of that friendship and the sharing of the work with them in hospital and church is a memory beyond price.

Elspeth (Crofts) Browne *served in Taiwan from 1961 till 1970, working in the Changhua Hospital. She returned to the UK for family reasons and married the Revd Percy Browne, sharing in his ministry at Bolton, Walsall and Wyke.*

After two years full time language study in Taiwan I began to work in the Changhua Christian Hospital which had been founded in 1896 and had developed slowly during the years of Japanese occupation of Taiwan. Missionaries made up 1% of the total staff number and my first task was as a joint sister in a surgical ward, alongside a Taiwanese sister who was a kind and subtle mentor. The standard of care given to the 100 patients was good but the physical environment left much to be desired. This was a challenging and fascinating time, as a new 400 bed hospital was already planned and began to be erected alongside the original buildings. It was not an easy time for either the patients or the staff who had to tolerate the noise and the general disturbance.

At that time the hospital did not train nurses but that soon changed and after a year as a ward sister I transferred to the newly revived School of Nursing. This was run by an American nurse assisted by a Chinese nurse and me plus several lecturers who contributed special subjects. The three different cultures blended surprisingly easily and we worked hard to adopt the best parts of the methods of three continents. Our student nurses did not pay for their training, uniform or accommodation (which was very unusual for Taiwan) but we considered they earned these by their work in the wards. During their first year they were in their classroom six hours a day and in the wards for one and a half hours ; the second year the balance was about half and half and in their third year they had classes just one day a week.

As well as the classes you would expect (practical nursing, anatomy, physiology and so on) our students had to learn and speak English. We often had English and American patients and for all patients the doctors' notes were written in English; obviously a nurse who could not read the doctor's instructions was not safe. The students were taught most subjects in Mandarin Chinese, the official national language, but I taught practical nursing skills using Taiwanese, the language most people used at home. When the students worked in the wards they would need Taiwanese, Mandarin and English to be able to talk to their patients; Japanese was also useful at times to be able to talk to older people from the aboriginal tribes.

I hope it goes without saying that Christian education and Bible study were an essential part of the curriculum. Every day opened with

Prayers and a charming older lady was invited to conduct a Bible class. She was not otherwise part of the hospital staff, in order to minimise any feeling the students might have that they were being pressurised into becoming Christian. The hospital Chaplain also worked with the students and a high percentage of them became and remained Christians. The example of Christian service set by the hospital staff of all grades had a long-lasting effect on many who came into contact with it.

Changhua Christian Hospital was one of several run by the Presbyterian Church in Taiwan. In the 1960s it was the only large hospital in the County, though there was other Christian medical work and I became slightly involved with some of it. One project was a skin clinic with about a dozen in-patients plus three to four hundred out-patients one day a week. Many of the latter were children with rashes, fungal infections, boils, eczema, dermatitis and all the problems which often accompany a poor diet and inadequate housing. The clinic was run by a Danish Lutheran nurse who was my neighbour and friend and she was the only qualified nurse working there. I used to offer myself as a deputy if she needed to be away for a few days, though never to run the out-patients' clinic! All the in-patients had leprosy in varying degrees of severity and deformity, and in the clinic they found a welcome, treatment, practical help for their problems and they became members of an accepting, caring community. I valued getting to know both the staff and the patients and I still treasure and use the wedding presents they made for me.

Another Christian group was a small community of Maryknoll Sisters. They were headed by a dynamic and amazing nun who was a doctor, the others were nurses or social workers. Their main outreach was to the many mothers and young children in Changhua. Sister Antonia Maria had her own way of doing her bit to improve the diet of toddlers, most of whom were undernourished. She hired a couple of teen-agers to cook large pots of a kind of porridge made from cracked wheat, and before she saw the child he or she was required to eat a bowl of this with milk and sugar added. She knew that if she handed out "the makings" the wheat would probably have gone to the hens! Sister Antonia Maria also persuaded several of her doctor friends from the States to come to Taiwan for a month - at their own expense - to treat patients and teach doctors. Usually they were based in Changhua Christian Hospital as that was where the necessary facilities were easily available. Denominational boundaries were not significant to any of us.

During my last year in Taiwan the ways the hospital was involved in nurse education changed radically and I found myself with less work to do in that department. This coincided with the absence of anyone carrying out a supervisory house-keeper role in the hospital, so I offered to fill the gap. It was an interesting experience and involved me in a variety of activities, all of which had a direct bearing on nursing care. Florence Nightingale had shown in Scutari that after just two months of her control of standards in the kitchen, the laundry and in ward cleaning, the death rate fell from 40% to 4%. During those early weeks she gave no nursing care. I cannot claim any such achievements but I am convinced basic hygiene has a direct effect on patient recovery.

My work in Taiwan was never dull and often challenging. It had an unexpected postscript when my husband and I were invited to join the hospital's centenary celebrations - now a state-of-the-art 1500-bed hospital built on the site of my old home. While there I met about thirty of my former students, all cheerful and contented women and all leading useful lives. Some are still nursing and some have moved to other work, including the ordained ministry. My husband had become ill en route to Taiwan and spent five days in the hospital cared for by a younger generation of nurses for the most part. The friendliness and compassion of all the staff shone out and despite our anxieties we are agreed it was a happy time. I doubt if it is possible to pay a greater tribute than that to the staff of any hospital and I am proud to have worked alongside them.

John Whitehorn *responded to the appeal for missionaries to work in the fast-growing church among the indigenous 'mountain' people of Taiwan. He had studied classics, theology and phonetics at Cambridge, and after his appointment a further year of Japanese at the London School of Oriental and African Studies. With his wife,* **Elizabeth**, *he served in Taiwan from 1951 to 1970, much of his time devoted to the translation of the Bible into the Paiwan language.*

After arriving in Taiwan I stayed in Tainan for six months and received some orientation into the ways of the Presbyterian Church in Taiwan and the English Presbyterian Mission. I did some further study of Japanese which was still a *lingua franca* among all but the younger generation, and visited various parts of the island to see people involved in the church's work with the indigenous 'mountain' peoples.

It was decided that I should learn the language of the Paiwan people who lived within the area of the South Synod, to which the E.P.Mission was linked. My colleagues reluctantly agreed that after only six months of orientation and with no knowledge of Taiwanese I could live in Pintong, the nearest large town to the Paiwan mountain area. There were a few Western missionaries of other missions living there, and for many years there was a tradition that all Protestant missionaries in the town met for prayers every week. But I was expected to go back to Tainan about every three weeks.

The Taiwanese minister of the old church in Pintong had been the pioneer in taking the Gospel to the Paiwan people and sending a Biblewoman to live in a Paiwan village. He arranged for a young Paiwan man, Gilgilav from Valuru, the village where the first Paiwan church had been founded, to act as my informant. We had Japanese in common, and from him I gradually learnt some Paiwan vocabulary and syntax. With him I visited most areas of the mountains where Paiwans lived to compare the dialects. We did not make very good arrangements for Gilgilav's housing, but built a shack for him in the grounds of a new Taiwanese church in Pintong.

After about eighteen months another young man from Valuru, Pari, was appointed as preacher at a clinic run by the Mennonites; and as he was brighter he took over from Gilgilav as my informant. Before I went on furlough in 1954 we had produced a small hymnbook and a 'Christian's Handbook' containing translations of parts of Mark's Gospel.

I returned in 1956 with Elizabeth and son David. For a year we lived in Tainan and Elizabeth and I learned Taiwanese. Then we moved to Pintong and I resumed translation work, checking what Pari had translated from Japanese into Paiwan. I was now an ordained minister, so I was given the job of going round Paiwan churches administering baptism and the Lord's Supper about twice a year in each village. This continued for the rest of my time.

At the General Assembly meeting in 1958 I made a speech saying that the Church should appoint a full-time executive secretary for the indigenous peoples' churches. I was invited to be an associate secretary, based in Taipei. Our family move to Tamsui and then to Taipei. When I persuaded a Taiwanese minister to take over the job in 1960 we moved back to Pintong, and I resumed Paiwan translation work with Pari. 'Mark' and 'Acts' were published and also a new hymnbook. Elizabeth helped as a doctor in the Christian hospital run by the Norwegians. The children, all in due course, went to the kindergarten at the old church.

After furlough in 1961-62 I was asked by Ko Chun-beng

(C.M.Kao) to take his place as principal of the Giok-san (Yu-shan) Bible School for indigenous peoples while he went abroad for further study. It was supposed to be a half-time job, allowing me to continue with some Paiwan translation work. But a big building programme made it a full-time job. There were 100 students from ten different language groups. Other things which took my time were the all-island 'mountain work' committee and the united Mission Council of English, Canadian and American missionaries linked to the Presbyterian Church in Taiwan. We lived for a year in Hualien town and then on the beautiful lake-side site of the Bible School. The children loved the free open-air life, and Elizabeth continued to teach them. There was an Agricultural School alongside the Bible School and that's where David got his love of agriculture.

In 1965 we were able to return to Pintong, and Pari and I produced translations of more books of the New Testament. All our drafts were checked by a group representing different Paiwan dialects and by a group of ministers who could read Chinese and/or Japanese. Drafts all had to be re-typed on a typewriter specially adapted for an alphabetic script adapted from the Chinese phonetic script used in the first year or two of Chinese primary schools.

When Elizabeth's cancer was first diagnosed in 1966 we returned to England. She recovered enough for me to go back to Pintong in 1967 to try to finish the New Testament in three years. Elizabeth and the three younger children came out to Pintong for the middle year of the three, while David went to Eltham College.

In 1970 I returned to England with a final draft and typed it up. After some delays the New Testament in Paiwan with Mandarin Chinese side by side was published in 1973.

In 1984 the Paiwan Presbytery asked the United Bible Societies to make it possible for the Old Testament to be translated into Paiwan. Cukar, a theological college graduate who could read some English as well as Chinese, was chosen as chief translator and other ministers formed a review committee, including representatives of some other denominations. Pari had died by now. I was asked to act as advisor. In the more relaxed political atmosphere it was now possible to use a romanised script, and my first job was to key in the New Testament on a word-processor.

Between 1986 and 1991 I made four trips to Taiwan to consult with Cukar and the committee. The last one was seven months in Taiwan and Singapore to finalise the text of the Shorter Bible, comprising about two-thirds of the Old Testament (the selections being made by the United Bible

Societies) and a revised New Testament. On these trips I stayed with an old friend in Pintong, a member of the Swedish Mission Covenant Church in Finland.

After unexplained delays the Shorter Bible was finally published in 1993 and I was invited to attend the thanksgiving service. Six thousand copies were printed and about 2,000 were sold quickly, but I hear that not very many more have been sold since. The government has done a U-turn and decided to promote 'mother tongues', but it remains to be seen whether the younger generation will want to read literature in their own language.

Peter and Agnes Storey. *Peter Storey served as an agricultural missionary in Taiwan from 1963 to 1979 and then in Nepal for a further twelve years. Whilst studying at Selly Oak he met Agnes Watson, a Methodist nurse. When Peter went to Taiwan, Agnes went to her work in India but in 1966 they were married in Taiwan. The following are some extracts from a longer account he has written of his missionary experience.*

I had wanted to travel most of the way to Formosa (Taiwan) as a co-driver/mechanic for a mission Landrover and trailer which was going overland to Malaysia. However, as I had to start the September Chinese language course in Taipei there was no time. I had to fly.

After flying over the South China Sea and then the Taiwan Straits I had my first view of Taiwan; first the coastal plains and then the mountains which cover two-thirds of the island. As we flew north over the mountains, Walter Carruthers, with whom I was travelling, said, 'Well, that is where you will be working, those are the people you have come to help'. Looking at the steep slopes and seeing the fields on them my heart dropped, how could I help them, it seemed crazy to try and farm such slopes yet they were doing just that. I felt that the most realistic thing was for me to take the next plane home. But - God had chosen me to serve the 'mountain' people - and, as Harold Wickings, my Selly Oak tutor had taught me, when we sincerely ask God for wisdom he will give it even when the situation seems hopeless.

We were met at the airport by the Rev. Ng Bu-tong, the General Secretary of the Presbyterian Church in Taiwan. Bu-tong asked me my English name and on the way into Taipei decided on my Chinese name, so I was christened for the second time. I became Su Bi-De.

We went to the Canadian Presbyterian compound. After lunch I was told to rest under a rattling ceiling fan. It was too hot and sticky to sleep, but soon I was roused from musing about my future by the sound of what

Pilgrims in Mission Memories: Taiwan

seemed to be sick bagpipes and drums. The tune I realised was roughly, 'Show me the way to go home'. Later a similar band passed by along Chung Shan Pei Lu (Middle Mountain North Road) outside; this time the tune was a Chinese tune followed by 'It's a long way to Tipperary'. I asked what the bands were for and was told, "Oh, they are funeral processions"! That cheered me up as I wondered if the band leaders had a sense of humour. I wondered also if they used the same tune for weddings, and later found that they did; they just speeded up the beat.

At my first morning at the Language Institute the director informed us that we were already in typhoon condition 3 and as typhoon 'Gloria' was expected to hit that night he did not expect to see us the following day. He was right! During the night even the re-inforced concrete building was shaken by the strength of the typhoon. When it was light I could see the shacks in the street outside being blown to pieces. It was not raining, rather it was as if buckets of water were constantly being thrown downward and sideways. The damage and flooding was terrible in Taipei but nothing to what I saw later in the countryside. Villages were buried by landslides or washed away by the flooding rivers. Sixty-seven inches of water fell in one day, the heaviest for 18 years. That was my water baptism in Taiwan. In my time there I experienced three other bad typhoons as well as several normal ones.

I think I was the worst language student in the language school. In order to try to learn Chinese I needed a punishing routine. I would get up at about 7.00 a.m., wash and have prayers and bible study, go out for breakfast and then to language school. After language school finished in the afternoon I would go to my room, write half an aerogramme to Agnes, and go for a run along the canal. Then go out to eat, make some Horlicks, have prayers and go to bed till my alarm clock woke me at midnight. I would then have a drink of coffee to wake me up and have three or four hours of language study, then more Horlicks and try to sleep. With so much noise outside during the day, firecrackers from weddings and other celebrations, vehicle horns and the clop clop clop of wooden clogs under my window, that time of night was the only time I could concentrate.

For the last six months of my language study it was decided that I should move to Tainan to learn something of the E.P. work. I was repeatedly told how the other E.P. missionaries had such good language, which did not do a lot for my ego. There were other ways in which I realised how my colleagues, past and present, were appreciated. The Chinese and the Taiwanese have a tradition, a day when the graves of the ancestors are swept and cleaned. The Taiwanese Christians have kept the custom and one day I went to the cemetery as one of the representatives of the English Presbyterian Mission. We were not allowed to clean the graves of the missionaries, they were very reverently cleaned by the Taiwanese Christians, and the cleaning was followed by moving speeches in which they expressed their gratitude for all the missionaries. During our earlier orientation course Dan Beeby had told us how when he had asked what the Taiwanese would most want of him, they had said, "We want your bones" - a colourful way of saying that they wanted the missionaries to give their lives rather than just a few years of service.

After the main language training was finished I went to the east of Taiwan, to a combined campus of the Yu Shan Bible School for tribal pastors and the Yu Shan Agricultural Centre which gave a one year course in agriculture to selected village representatives. As the language for all official teaching was Mandarin most of the students were young men. However, one I selected was older and like me had limited Chinese. We would read out to him the Examination questions and he would reply orally. Within six months of his return home, we received letters from his village and even neighbouring villages saying agricultural production had increased by 65% since his return; the improvement continued.

At first I was on one of the teaching teams which rotated. We would teach for two weeks and then go out to visit graduate students in their villages, scattered over the mostly mountainous tribal area. We would talk with them about their successes and problems, and discuss how to improve things. Then we would invite others to join in for discussion and mutual advice. We would give training talks and demonstrations as needed and ask them how we could help them to help themselves. Later I was in charge of the training farm and students' practical training.

In our second term we were first called to the Tayal tribe in the north-west to develop agricultural extension work, and later to the central East Coast area with three pilot villages, one each of the Taroko, Bunun and Amis tribes. This developed into the East Taiwan Aborigines Agricultural Service project covering 350 kilometres from north to south and about 40 wide, and ranging from tropical sea-level to temperate climate at 11,000 feet. It extended from livestock training and health to fish farming, rice and vegetables to fruit trees and wood mushrooms; intermediate technology to co-operative marketing and retailing. The marketing developed to 47 large lorry loads of produce per year.

It was stimulating but exhausting. It was particularly pleasing to be told by tribal pastors that our work gave their work credibility; that they could talk about the love of God for the tribal people and people could see it. It was most rewarding to see the tribal people gaining confidence and become as good or better than the Taiwanese farmers. They were quicker to take up new methods and had learnt to trust our work and advice. Our staff were so good, were all tribal, and we first tried things properly and showed the people respect.

During these years Agnes was kept busy with teaching our three children; two would be having home school with Agnes while the other was at Chinese school, and then after lunch they would change round. In the evening they had their Chinese school homework to do. When the eldest, Anne, was eleven she went to the American missionary boarding-school over the mountains in Taichung.

We are grateful for the privilege we had of serving tribal people of Taiwan through the English Presbyterian Mission. We have since served in Nepal for twelve years and spent five years researching and writing seven books on agriculturally related issues, two of which are published and very much appreciated. One just completed shares the lessons and observations of myself and others on how to have 'Appropriate Rural Development'. Sadly so much so-called rural development is hindering real and sustainable development, undermining the future and destroying the environment which God has given and on which rural people depend.

Walter and Doreen Carruthers served as teachers in Taiwan from 1957 to 1966. In that year they returned to the UK with their two children, and continued in their profession till taking early retirement in 1986.

Long Ago and Far Away

Oh! the intense summer heat and humidity. You shower, dry and put on the prickly heat powder but it becomes prickly heat paste as it touches your perspiring skin. You can't really communicate experiences like that to deputation audiences, or at least you can't without getting arrested. The same is true of a lot of your experiences.

Speaking to congregations, you get more and more depressed at your inability to communicate the real sensations of your life as a member of a sister church, still less the real life of your Taiwanese friends. You are emotionally disabled at leaving those friends to come back to England, and you have changed ineradicably since you went out.

Thirty-one years later we still feel that we have returned to a foreign country. The multi-cultural influx doesn't seem to have made that much of an impression on congregational life. The general sense of the world beyond Dover is weak. Maybe the focus on Europe has redirected minds which once felt closer to life which lay east of Suez.

Life, in our case working with Taiwanese people, was a greatly enriching experience. The knowledge that we had pulled up our tent-pegs to go and work with them led to an acceptance into Taiwanese people's lives with such warmth and affection that those who think of the Chinese as inscrutable must completely miss.

We were changed by our life in Taiwan and particularly by our work with Taiwanese, Christians and non-Christians. Intercourse with an ancient culture as rich or richer than that in which we had been brought up, gently remade us into what a colleague in England recently referred to as 'wily orientals'! Identification with an oppressed people who remained concerned for the oppressors, helped us to rethink the concept of patriotism and we came to see it as too often a thoughtless jingoism. Thirty-two years later this country's attitude to Europe (yes, Europe!) still festers in the same tainted subconscious.

Chinese culture tends to inculcate in men and women a deep feeling that they are not inherently inferior to other people and nations. Speechless for a long two years language study after arrival and stumbling in Taiwanese for more than three years thereafter, we lost some of the hyper-active drive that our culture develops in us and it was quite natural to find ourselves working as partners and co-learners with our Taiwanese co-workers. It is not only that they are much more familiar with their own society and culture than we can ever be, but that they confidently expect to find a way of living in the modern world that is consistent and rooted in their own way of life. In the next millennium the cultures of the West will no doubt experience the influence of that cultural confidence as it begins to impact on their own.

The establishment of self-governing and self-supporting churches was always one of the main purposes of the English Presbyterian Mission, and it is very satisfying that we are now members of churches which express this through their organisational structure in the Council for World Mission. This expresses symbolically and in practice what we can remember being argued about in the 1950s in the Presbyterian Fellowship of Youth National Councils and Summer Conferences. It seemed a far off aspiration then.

What, then, about our work in Taiwan? We taught English initially in Chang-Jung High School (*the Church Middle School*) in Tainan, then in Tainan University and Tainan Theological College, with a year in between teaching English in Tunghai University while Ivor Shepherd was on leave. Walter led the first two International Work Camps in Taiwan with Ko Chun-beng (C.M.Kao, later General Secretary of the Presbyterian Church in Taiwan) at the Giok-san (Yu-shan) Mountain Theological Institute, attended many youth conferences, conferences and committees on educational policy and practice, taught American servicemen's Bible Classes at the American Air Base (as part of a structured Church adult-education programme). Doreen, (an asterisk in the old Mission Prayer Manual) did very similar things until the children were born, but then taught the 'History of Western Culture' for two years as well as English conversation in Tainan University. We both worked for two years in the English Teaching programme at Tainan Theological College which did wonders in an intensive programme with a fully equipped language laboratory to develop the students' ability both to speak and cope with reading advanced theological textbooks in English. Students came freely to our house to listen to our records of English and American poets reading their own poetry. They practised their English conversation with us and now and then brought their own food to cook and gave us a party. They took us to sit through Chinese opera, explained Chinese attitudes to us and even occasionally wrote their own references for us to sign, just to save us time!

There was always plenty to do and most of what we were involved in meant trying to respond within very different cultural contexts. We still come out with Chinese, Japanese and Taiwanese words which express better what we want to say than English. Walter even became Mission Treasurer for a short time, doing accounts in four currencies and the different exchange rates for all of them. This was before electronic calculators.

We took out our NSU Quickly mopeds and enjoyed zooming all over Tainan city on them for our first few years. Taiwan (much changed now I hear) then had traffic which tended to use the centre of the road to travel in both directions. Many of the myriad cyclists were then wearing simple wooden clogs kept on the feet by plastic straps. When they fell off their feet, there ensued a graceful ballet as they swooped round the road in decreasing circles until they could pop the foot through the plastic strap without dismounting. Crossroads became scenes of slow chaos as thirty or forty bikes piled up and people got to their feet, popped their clogs on and bowed by way of apology to all and sundry. It made for exciting driving in powered vehicles.

Life in Taiwan has greatly changed since we were there. It has changed greatly here since 1966 when we came back. The struggle to discover God's purposes for us whether there or here is not all that different however different the context may be or become.

Margaret Barclay, *a science graduate, was appointed in 1957 to teach in the Presbyterian Girls' School in Tainan and served there till 1973, when she returned to the UK and continued her teaching career.*

It took six weeks to reach Taiwan by sea, changing boats in Hong Kong. I arrived in the middle of a Mission Council meeting and was confused to find so many different kinds of Presbyterian missionaries. As well as English and Canadian Presbyterians, there were Southern Presbyterians, Northern Presbyterians, United Church of Canada, United Presbyterians, Reformed Church of America and so on.

My bewilderment increased when I reached Tainan and gradually discovered that all the Formosans had two names. I had heard of the School Principal as Mr Liu (his Mandarin name) but now everyone spoke of him as Mr Lau (his Formosan name). Rather dreading any form of language study, my dismay increased on discovering that I had to learn both Formosan and Mandarin (the official language for education).

Most of my time was spent in school. My memories of teaching 'English Conversation' are of large classes, sometimes more than sixty. In the long hot and humid summers it was difficult to keep the girls awake, let alone staying awake myself.

English teaching was based on American pronunciation and spelling - so I sometimes wondered if I was confusing the girls more than helping them. However, many girls enjoyed the classes and there were colleges who liked to get our girls because they spoke 'English-English'.

As my subject is Biology, I was very glad to be involved in some Biology teaching. I was fortunate to have a Formosan colleague who was not only a good naturalist, knowing all the local fauna and flora, but also a good friend. We tried to expand practical work, which had to be very highly organised because of the large classes. With no bunsen burners, I got quite expert in handling alcohol lamps. Helping to focus numerous microscopes became quite hectic!

We were also involved in developing Field work and used to take groups of girls into the foothills where we lived in a cabin in the middle of a bamboo forest near a village called Koan-tz-ling. For some of these teenage girls, it was their first experience away from home. We took our own food and the girls did the cooking. We slept on the floor on Japanese matting called tatami. We travelled cheaply on local trains and buses, taking microscopes, fishing nets and all the other apparatus and equipment that we required.

Beside the cabin was a small river, so we had plenty of different habitats to study; bamboo forest, paddy fields, fruit tree and ginger plantations and even a mountain to climb, 1234 metres high. Returning home we would examine, identify and discuss our finds, trying to draw conclusions from our results. Then an evening meal under the stars, prayers, stories, singing and bed.

Rather less successful were my attempts at teaching Religious Education. Members of classes ranged from ardent Christians to aggressive non-Christians, with a great deal of passive indifference in between. Officially, RE did not exist in the curriculum, so it all had to be rather low key. Bible study was tolerated, but without much enthusiasm. But the girls loved music, so I tried to build the lessons around some form of religious music. Lessons all began well when I entered the classroom with a gramophone instead of a pile of Bibles.

The Christians wanted to start the lessons with a prayer. So I compromised with an English prayer. Each lesson began by singing, "God be in my head, and in my understanding......" The words were simple enough for all to understand and the lessons began with a prayer so everyone was happy.

But one year my class was not musical and the gramophone produced even less enthusiasm than the Bibles. So I introduced the social side of the work of the Church ....Hospitals, Leprosy Clinics, work with Blackfoot disease and so forth. One lesson I even gave out newspaper cuttings instead of Bibles. All this was trying to introduce the idea of Christian service and this made more sense to many of them.

I made many friends in Taiwan amongst my missionary colleagues, amongst the girls I taught, amongst my fellow teachers in the schools and, of course, in the Church.

I want to finish with a few of my impressions of the Church, the Presbyterian Church in Taiwan. Although only a small proportion of the population were Christian, the churches were large and well filled for services. Churches were growing. Agenda for General Assembly showed a wide range of different activities. People read the Bible regularly and really knew it well. Giving in the Church was very generous. There was hope and enthusiasm. People prayed, and believed firmly in the power of prayer. As an example, once when I was ill a girl came to visit me. I knew there was something wrong with our conversation but I couldn't quite work out what was missing. So I was not surprised when she returned the next day with a friend. She said, "Teacher, yesterday I wanted to pray for you because you were ill, but I am not very good at praying so I brought a friend. She is much better at praying than I am. Her friend led us in prayer and then they departed. I was left feeling very humble.

I learnt a great deal from my friends in Taiwan, probably more than I ever taught them. While I was glad to return to England, it is certainly very different here. Perhaps part of me is in Taiwan and always will be.

Ivor and Joan Shepherd served in Taiwan from 1958 to 1995. Ivor was sent out by the OMC in response to a request from the Board of the newly founded Tunghai University, and was appointed a lecturer in English. He served in this appointment for thirty-seven years, until retirement and return to the UK in 1995.

Home and Family
Table of Contents
You at that end stand arranging flowers;
I at this end sit composing verse.
Creation is not yours or mine, but ours.

The waiting minutes seem like lingering hours.
I by the altar formal vows rehearse;
You at that end stand arranging flowers.

From birth to graduation time devours
A hundred birthdays - daughters grow, disperse.
Creation is not yours or mine but ours.

In our home tea and talk pass happy hours.
Some at this end right the universe;
You at that end stand arranging flowers.

I teach and toil in plaque-stained ivory towers;
You ease things - hostess, confidante and nurse.
Creation is not yours or mine, but ours.

And with the passing years, sunshine and showers,
I'll still sit here at this end writing verse,
While you at that end stand arranging flowers.
Creation is not yours or mine, but ours.

People and Places
               Artificial Hands
The politician's stiff, smooth, plastic paw
waves to cheering crowds below.

The old street vendor's hinged steel claw
serves hot soup to a man and his child.

              Village Storyteller
At the temple gate
he waits to tell old tales. But
now they watch new ones

              On Shihtoushan
Dawn. A cypress tree
black against the grey light.
Nuns chant, "Amitofo."

              On Yangmingshan
Alone on the hill
a country lass at work
sings "Coming through the Rye."

             In Changhua Hospital
Wedding fireworks outside
drown a woman's weeping
for her new — dead child.

Faith and Worship
              Easter Morning
Seen through the altar window
three linked kites - red, blue, yellow
rise swiftly in the strong wind

Taut across the black-squared panes
one white cord
glistens in the bright sunlight.

    Spirit
Louder than words
a bird cries and beats the plate glass
trying to fly free.

    Elements
We take bread and wine.
On the altar window
a spider takes a fly.

    Capella Lucis*
It is Christmas Eve.

The Chapel is in darkness, save for one great candle
on the altar.

All the people stand holding small candles, as yet unlit.

Three people come forward and light their candles
from the single flame.

One light has become four.

The three flamebearers turn and walk away,
one to the choir and two to the centre aisle.

They move from row to row, lighting the candles
of those at the row-ends.

These bend to light their neighbours' candles,
and they in turn do the same.

So drops become streams, and then a fountain,
cascading into every corner of the Chapel, until
all is awash with light.

High above the people, reflected in the tall window
behind their heads, shine the candles of the choir
as they sing, "Glory to God in the highest, and on
earth, peace, goodwill toward men."

The doors are already open, and row by row,
the people, all flamebearers now, flow out of the
Chapel, at first in one broad stream, then spreading
into pools and trickles, carrying the light
down the hill and away.

In the Chapel, still and quiet now, the flame
of the single great candle burns clear and bright

* Chapel of Light / The Luce Chapel, Tunghai

More People and Places

    In a Taipei Courtyard
Drying clothes fly from
dragon-twined flagpoles
of a long-dead mandarin.

    Urban Skyline
On curved green-tile roofs
saucer-eyed, glass-scaled dragons
writhe in playful pairs

On square grey tower-blocks
pot-bellied plastic cisterns
squat in sullen rows.

    By the Freeway
A half-built temple's
bell or drum shaped windows stare
blankly at the cars.

In a Department Store
Dark-robed, heads shaven,
Nuns gaze at coiffured dummies
in smart, bright dresses.

On the Road to School
A butterfly flits
past a book-laden child.
She chases it in vain.

Students and Teaching

Composition Class, December 21st
She writes the assigned
Christmas tale, humming alto
to next door's carols.

Bilingual Wit
Our students named their snack-bar, "Carpe Diem" —
a fitting tag to spice their bread and cheese.
When we realised the rest,
We were even more impressed —
the phrase means "coffee-shop" in Taiwanese!

Keys
(To my students as I retire)
I keep my keys in this old, faded case.
The leather's torn, the press-stud doesn't catch,
half the hooks are missing, so the rest
must hold two keys. It's well-worn, but it serves.

The case holds seven assorted keys in all:
for my house, department, office, P.O.Box,
the one for the teachers' washroom, and two whose use
I've long forgotten — I keep them anyway.

None of these keys go with me; some, with the case,
will be discarded; some passed on to those
who'll soon replace me in my home and work.
And I will find new keys for a new life.

But you?
What keys will you find, forge or be given here,
soon to be cased in a bright new Tunghai diploma?
Which keys will you discard and which retain?

Which will open doors at once and serve
a daily purpose through the years to come?
Which will bend or break at the first try,
and have to be thrown away in rage or tears?

Which one now seems to fit no lock you know of
and so will remain unused, perhaps for years,
until one day you come across the door
this one key fits - a vital door for you?

The day I was twenty-one, as a formal gift
I received my home's front-door key, a sign
I was now free to come and go at will.
Here may you all receive the keys you need
to unlock the doors you choose in your future life.

Postscript:
We have returned to Taiwan twice as guests of generous Chinese friends, renewing old ties and revisiting old haunts.

On the second occasion I was invited (as in the past) by a former colleague to teach his British Literature class (once my freshmen, now his seniors) to sing Blake's "Jerusalem." We sang this and then went on to Gilbert and Sullivan and Burns, ending with "Auld Lang Syne," crossed hands and all. Memories.

After teacher training and experience followed by two more years missionary training at Carey Hall, Selly Oak, **Alvinza Riddoch** *served in Yungchun, South Fujian, 1946-1948, in Singapore, 1949-1952, and in Taiwan from 1952 to 1973, when she returned to the UK on retirement.*

I left Selly Oak in the summer of 1943 but as there was no open road to China, I was handed over to the Women's Home Church Committee and appointed to a new 'charge' in Huyton. There I was 'set apart' by the

Liverpool Presbytery in the backyard of an empty shop on a new housing estate, to build up the family of God amongst a scattering of people who had been bombed out of Bootle. In the few months I was there I made friends, found great difficulties in renting a room in council houses, and was amazed at the loving service of the Revd Copland Simmonds, Chairman of the Liverpool Church Extension Committee, who came with his wife and gave musical concerts to our small group of worshippers, and invited his 'church sister' to 'take a bath' in the manse. In September an experienced church sister, Branwen Jones, took over from me and I was seconded to Regent Square Church in London, where I was able to work with Children's Camps and Fellowship Groups which still continued in spite of reduced rations, bombing raids and the new terrors of V1 and V2 rocket bombs. When one of the last of these destroyed Church House and much of Regent Square Church I was able to scramble out of the wreckage and with help prepared a room for worship on the coming Sunday.

I finally sailed for China in March, 1946. Unlike many missionary friends who at that time experienced the rigours of travelling on troopships, the Blue Funnel steamer on which we sailed by New York and San Francisco to Shanghai provided a first experience of freedom from rationing and the rediscovered enjoyment of good food, for which the thirteen missionaries on board daily gave thanks. After ten days stay in Shanghai at the Lester Memorial Hospital, kindness of the London Missionary Society, and a further stay in Hong Kong of the same kind, plus more health checks and injections, I finally reached Amoy on board the consular yacht. It had been a long wait to get there but in the end I was blessed with good companions and comfortable journeying.

Daisy Pearce and Margaret Beattie had arrived together a few weeks previously and met me in Amoy. Daisy had already served one tour at the Hoai Tek Kindergarten Training School and knew her way around. Since their arrival she had collected enough furniture, kept secure during the Japanese occupation, to furnish a house for our use. Finding a suitable language teacher during the summer holiday time was not so easy but I had three students every morning to teach me to read and tell stories in the vernacular. From visiting Christian families in the afternoon I learnt more practical things, such as cooking in the Chinese way, which stood me in good stead in later years. It was not until after Chinese New Year, 1947, that I reached Yungchun, walking there from Chuanchow with Boris and Clare Anderson, even more recent arrivals and making their first visit. We stayed overnight at a country chapel but found that none of us had adequate language to make requests or deal with the 'carrying coolie' who had my bags on his carry-pole. My American Methodist colleague in Yungchun, Wenona Jett, was a precious gift to our Mission. She helped me with the language, took me visiting in nearby villages, gave me many opportunities to teach in school and church and at outdoor meetings. In the summer, we took an exciting journey into the mountains with a Singapore evangelist, visiting the churches who had no ministers. Most days we walked six to ten miles, from one family home to another. As we walked the evangelist and I told each other an Aesop's fable - each in the other's language. At night, I listened to his sermons, tried to discover where they differed from the previous night, and learned many phrases which told of God's love, and the coming of His Kingdom. I also developed malarial blood, which wasn't discovered until much later. This was a very happy time, walking in mountain country, discovering wayside flowers, eating fruits picked from the trees by the paths. But it was also a time of growing unrest, a time when currency halved its value every week. Local bandits and communists became more and more active until one evening, in the spring of 1948, Wenona and I, carrying small handbags for the three-day journey through the rapids to Chuanchow, walked on to a river launch packed with pottery. The communists entered the small town of Yungchun and I never returned.

  A long period of injections and rest in Chuanchow was followed by an early furlough to recover my health and hopefully return to Yungchun. On our way to China, in the autumn of 1949, Christina Holmes and I reached Singapore to learn that we were to stay there until the situation in China was clearer. So I did, helping Monica Sirkett in the Kuo Chuan Girls' School, teaching in English but also sharing in the life of an active Amoy-speaking congregation. But just before Christmas, 1951, the home committee decided that I should be transferred to Taiwan. I spent a very happy Chinese New Year month in Hong Kong with my friends at the London Missionary Society while I waited for a visa to Taiwan, now under the Chinese government of Chiang Kai Shek.

  By 1952 the Tainan Theological College had reopened and Daisy Pearce was invited by Shoki Ko to open a kindergarten teacher training course under the College umbrella. There was a keen demand for such teachers in the already existing kindergartens and after the Doubling the Church Movement began in 1955 this greatly increased. In due course I took over from Daisy. The training was upgraded to three years with students more closely integrated into the theological and Biblical courses. The churches realized that their kindergartens should be centres for evangelism, since most of the children came from non-Christian homes. In the villages, all teachers were welcomed in pupils' homes, and many grandmothers dared to visit the kindergartens to discover the joys of book learning. I found it exciting when the churches from all the Southern presbyteries wanted kindergarten teachers who could not only take charge of fifty 3-6 year-olds, but play the harmonium and lead or sing in the choirs, and help the women's organisation to spread the gospel in their own extension programme. At first, remuneration was a problem, but the churches realised that these young women were precious in the eyes of the congregation, and a degree from the Tainan Theological College was a good part of a dowry.

The years passed quickly with teaching, and leading conferences for kindergarten teachers in vacations. Trained and untrained teachers met for five or six days in the largest church in each area, and various aspects of children's development, and patterns of learning were discussed. New ways of teaching reading and writing Chinese characters were practised as well as singing of new songs and dancing and rhythmic exercises. All who participated were Christian teachers and usually we were led in Bible Study by the local minister. The Kindergarten Teachers Association linked up with similar organizations in Japan and Korea, and several times teachers were exchanged at the conferences.

In this way I felt very much at home in most of the churches, since there were graduates in all presbyteries. Many of the girls married fellow-students from the College and weddings were a feature in all the holidays. Some of the graduates went on to study in Japan, others went to the USA with their husbands, though the government was slow to give passports to more than one family member at the same time. I learned much about children's learning patterns from spending hours with my own students who each spent several hours weekly in the Observation Rooms built into the Practice School. It was sometimes difficult to control the grandmothers who watched their charges with avidity and shouted controlling remarks aloud!

By the end of the 1960s Tainan Theological College had enough well-trained and experienced teachers in my field. In 1969 I had accepted an invitation from the Revd Y.S.Wang, Principal of the Hsin Chu Bible School, to teach some courses there two days a week, and in 1970 it was agreed that I should move there. The Bible School taught Middle School and Mountain School graduates so that they could do extension work with country churches. Anna Chen returned from the USA and Dorothea Siao of the Philippines was appointed by the Presbyterian Church in the US to help strengthen the Christian Education Department. It was a time of great growth on that campus, and during that last term of service, among other things, it thrilled me to work with the young architect who designed the Practice School - with facilities for observing the children at play.

I returned to England in 1975 for retirement. It has been and still is a time of continued contacts and visits to and from former colleagues, friends, and graduates. It was a great thrill to be invited to the Baccalaureate Service in Elmhurst, Chicago when a former student received a doctorate for her work in education at the Hanil Theological College in Changju, Korea. Another dear friend, Rev. Minnie Lee, has recently returned to Taiwan from Brazil, where she led worship services in Japanese, Taiwanese or Mandarin almost every Sunday for more than twelve years. Now she is the Principal of the Tao Shan Seminary, which is largely financed by the Women's Committee of the Presbyterian Church in Taiwan. Ruth Chen has managed the School for Blind Children in Taichung county for more than twenty years, though we were together at its beginnings in the early fifties. Thinking of the countless families in churches in Taiwan and the USA who cherish photographs of their children holding their graduation certificates, I know that I'm privileged to have had a part to play in the work of the coming Kingdom.

Elizabeth Brown *served in Taiwan from 1961 to 1989, in Tainan and Taipei, as a teacher, in a Christian Student Centre, an administrator and chaplain. After training for the ministry in Taipei and Cambridge, she was ordained by the URC and served as a chaplain in Taipei. Following her return to the UK in 1989 she has continued that ministry in the universities at Leeds.*

"The Archbishop of York will be wearing his Convocation robes...."so I, as the United Reformed Church chaplain at the University of Leeds, will appear in layers of ministerial and academic dress as I lead the prayers before his Chaplaincy Sermon here this week. On such occasions I always feel that it is slightly surrealistic that an M.Div hood from Taiwan Theological College and Seminary should be bobbing about amidst more easily recognised trophies.

In writing this personal reminiscence I want primarily to focus on my time in the north, when I was living at Taiwan Theological College - first using it as a convenient base for my work as Assistant General Secretary at the General Assembly Offices in Taipei and then working as chaplain there. My M.Div studies overlapped both periods. How did I, after living for thirteen years in the south on the home ground of the English Presbyterian Mission, end up in 'the other place' - the centre of Canadian Presbyterian work.

My time at the General Assembly Office(1976-1984) coincided with one of the most difficult and yet glorious times for the Presbyterian Church in Taiwan. It issued the Declaration on Human Rights in 1977; Dr C.M.Kao, the General Secretary, was arrested in 1980 and not released from prison until 1985. During the whole of that time the authorities kept up a sustained onslaught on the church, especially on those who carried responsibility for the General Assembly. This affected me in a number of ways. For some time I was living under the threat of immediate arrest. My whereabouts and activities were the subject of official reports. For a considerable time I was refused renewal of my Residence Permit and could therefore have been deported at any minute. A succession of Acting General Secretaries varied greatly in the amount of time they were able to give to the office and there were occasions when, in order to keep things going, I had to carry more responsibility than was proper. But what was hardest to bear was that rumours discrediting me were being skilfully planted, especially in the south, so that whenever I went down to Tainan I no longer felt as if I was going home. During this prolonged stressful period my fellow members and elders at Chi Nan Presbyterian Church and friends at Taiwan Theological College, especially the Principal Dr I.S.Seah and his wife were a great support and comfort to me. He assured me that a job awaited me at the College whenever I wanted it.

Though I had felt called to the ministry of Word and Sacrament from undergraduate days, I also had a strong call to work in Taiwan and it was only in the early 1980s that I found a way of reconciling these by candidating for the ministry of the United Reformed Church and picking up available theological courses at the Night School of the Taiwan Theological College. Classes were on Tuesday and Thursday evenings and I found them stimulating and enjoyable. Keeping up with the reading and writing book reports and essays while working as Assistant General Secretary was not easy, though fortunately all my teachers had studied overseas and I was able to submit written work in English. At this distance of time I can't remember clearly which courses I did in the Night School and which I did in the day time, but I do recall desperately typing Old Testament reports at lunch time in the office, learning New Testament Greek vocabulary on city buses and even writing an essay on Pope Leo X in the bar of Kaohsiung Airport. These are all courses which you would find at any reputable Theological College, but it was immensely interesting to experience them in a Taiwanese culture, to gain Taiwanese insights and to benefit from courses such as Church and Society and Taiwanese Folk Religion which set the Gospel in its local setting. I remember one fascinating exercise when each student took a different family (I had the Chengs from Ta Tu) and researched its family tree. Then we put them all together and saw where they overlapped and intersected - ending up with a map of Taiwan church history spelt out in people. Interaction with fellow-students was an important contributory factor to this and I appreciated the community and friendship they offered. When I left Taiwan in 1989 one of them travelled a considerable distance to say goodbye to me and pray with me.

I left the General Assembly Office in 1984 and spent the academic year 1984-1985 in England at Westminster College, Cambridge and was ordained (after consultation between the Taiwan and the UK church authorities) in June 1985, returning to Taiwan that summer as chaplain to Taiwan Theological College and Seminary. I completed my degree work in the M.Div Department while teaching English in the undergraduate departments, but was not unique in this as two of my fellow-students were doing the same. I had continued to be deeply involved in local church activities at Chi Nan Presbyterian Church and when it was time for me to graduate I said to those who were in a small group Bible study there with me that as I didn't have any family members in Taiwan I would appreciate it if any of them who were free would come to the graduation and be my family. To my amazement, fourteen people came, some having taken the day off work. I was tremendously grateful to them for being there so I could share my day with them.

Does a Theological College need a chaplain? Nowadays most people would respond, "Of course." But when I began at Taiwan Theological College, the answer was not so clear. Surely with so many ministers on the teaching staff pastoral care for the students was being provided in abundance? But where something is everybody's job, it often doesn't get done. Not only that, the chaplain is responsible for the whole College community - gardeners, kitchen staff, secretaries and teachers as well as students. I well remember visiting the home of one of the non-Christian gardeners and sitting by his mother's coffin with the rest of the family.

There were nearly 300 students at the College when I was chaplain there. I managed to get a small office which was part of the student activity centre. It was noisy, but very accessible. I spent every evening there. Often students would drop in with text books and course materials which they didn't understand and use me as a tutor. I was happy to help when I could and this provided some 'camouflage' for students with personal problems who might otherwise have been shy about being seen to go into the chaplain's office. Many came in carrying books which were never opened once they were inside.

All theology departments have students for whom the academic study of theology is an unexpected shock, threatening to undermine their faith and temporarily knocking them off their feet. The chaplain who is apart from this academic process is in a position to help and support them. Similarly students who had broken the College rules or who had "lost their faith" felt at ease with someone who was not part of the disciplinary structure. A number of our M.Div students would get married just before coming to us. They faced a variety of problems all at the same time - adjusting to being married, financial problems, living in very confined married quarters with screaming babies, and so on. In our relatively small community students were sharing rooms and everybody tended to know everybody else's business. This was very hard for those who were just taking their first steps in making friends with the opposite sex. I remember a young man coming into my office one day, sitting down, bursting into tears and saying, "This is the only place in the College where I can weep."

I left Taiwan in 1989 to come to work in the universities in Leeds. It was a great joy to be invited back by Chi Nan Presbyterian Church in the spring of 1996 as part of their Centenary Celebrations. In the ten days I was there I was able to visit Tainan - and it felt like "coming home" again. And my visit to the General Assembly offices was full of delightful surprises when I found how many of the staff there had been students at Taiwan Theological College.

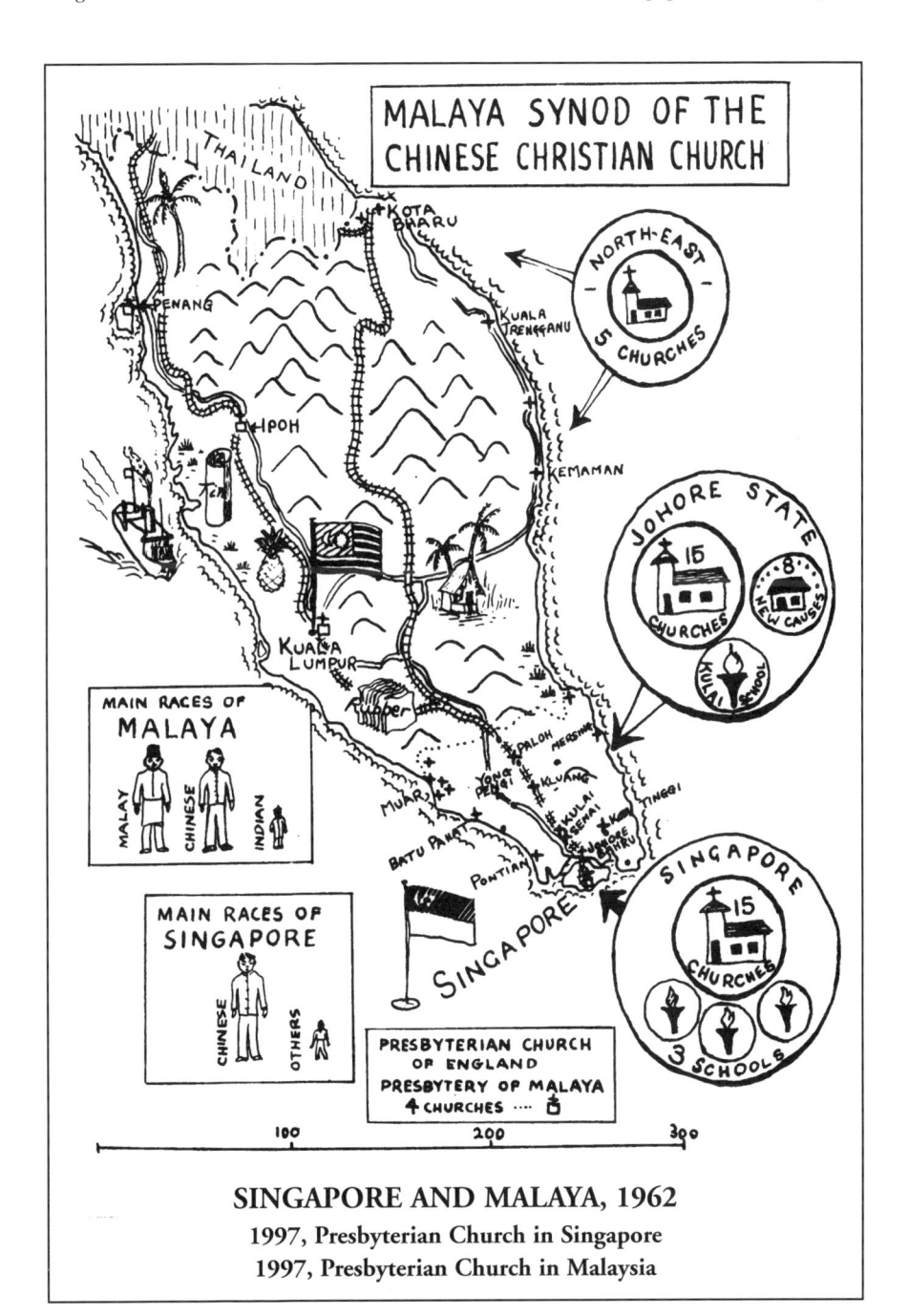

SINGAPORE AND MALAYA, 1962
1997, Presbyterian Church in Singapore
1997, Presbyterian Church in Malaysia

MEMORIES: SINGAPORE AND MALAYSIA

Monica Sirkett served as an educational missionary in Singapore from 1947 to 1972. Her colleague and friend, *Margaret Honey (nee Prestige)*, who served in the same Kuo Chuan Girls School from 1952 to 1956 and maintains close links with it to the present day, has written these memories of Monica.

Monica Sirkett went to Singapore in 1947 to re-establish the Presbyterian Girls' School founded originally in 1924, but closed during the Japanese occupation. When she arrived she found a large ramshackle house, damaged by bombing and with a leaking roof. The first Principal, Margaret Dryburgh had died in a Japanese internment camp in Sumatra together with Ann Livingston and Sabine Mackintosh and it was after these three Presbyterian missionaries, some of the real people behind the "Tenko" story and more recently, the film "Paradise Road", that the School Houses were named. Monica planned the development of the school with great care for details of this kind. There was a magnificent Flame of the Forest tree in the grounds and long after the old house had gone to make room for the new buildings, generations of girls played in its shade. It was this tree, and the Presbyterian emblem of the burning bush which inspired the school motto "Aflame for Truth".

Monica established a pattern of school life beginning each day with worship and she sought to fashion a school community with traditions which could be handed on, a school community which also had strong links with the local church. She saw the school as complementary to the church and a place where future leaders could be trained.

The 1950s were a time of development in English-speaking work within the Singapore/Malaya Synod of the Chinese Christian Church. As the demand for English-medium education increased so did the need for the establishment of English-speaking church activities. Under her leadership the Sunday School and the Youth Fellowship, inaugurated in 1951, attracting students from both the Presbyterian Boys' School and Kuo Chuan Girls' School grew and flourished. The small congregation which had begun meeting in the Boys School hall began to share the Zion Presbyterian Church. On the 27th January 1957 the Synod Executive raised Katong Presbyterian English-speaking preaching station to the status of a fully sanctioned charge with the Revd J R Shad as interim moderator. There was a membership of 51 and 30 adherents, 4 elders, 5 deacons, a Sunday School of 200 and a Youth Fellowship of 50. Early Session members included both teachers and former pupils of the Presbyterian Boys' School.

In this time of expansion in English-medium education in Singapore, the Christian schools, Catholic, Anglican, Methodist and Presbyterian, formed a vital part of the whole school system. The Government gave grants to them and funded 50 per cent of their building schemes. This meant a good deal of the money had to be raised by the schools themselves, so all kinds of fund-raising activities were organised. In those early days Monica inspired the girls, many of whom came from very humble backgrounds, and most of whom were not from Christian homes, to have a vision of a school to be proud of, a place where future generations of schoolgirls would have better and more splendid facilities. She contacted local business men for sponsorship and it was agreed that the school should be called Kuo Chuan Girls' commemorating the father of its chief benefactor.

In 1949 the old house was demolished and a new single storey building providing four new classrooms was erected. In 1950 enough money had been raised for four new classrooms, an office, a staffroom and the installation of modern sanitation and this new building was completed in 1951. Monica undertook a considerable amount of teaching. As the school grew with each annual intake of the primary first-year stage, the work towards the Senior Cambridge examination increased. She built up a devoted and capable staff, many of whom were committed Christians and she was also involved with supervision of students from the Teacher Training College. At this time, all school buildings were used twice over in the course of the day, the morning school from 7.30 and the afternoon school from 1.15. Staff taught in one session, but Monica was head of both morning and afternoon schools and was thus usually at her desk for twelve hours a day.

The next stage of development culminated in the building of the Assembly Hall, Domestic Science rooms and a school canteen. After twenty years, the first single storey building was demolished to make way for Science Laboratories, a Library and a separate Staffroom for the Secondary School teachers.

When Singapore became an independent republic within the Commonwealth, Monica became a Singapore Citizen, something of which she was intensely proud and a status which she was unwilling to relinquish. In 1972 she had to retire having reached the compulsory retirement age for School Principals at that time. She had worked tirelessly and with great devotion for 25 years to establish a fine school based on strong Christian principles. She was single-minded and very determined. She was extremely conscientious in everything she did in planning and preparation for both school and church work and development. She had a marvellous way with children, a great sense of fun and she was a splendid teacher. She had a vision of what could be achieved from very small beginnings and laid firm foundations. The vitality and success of both the primary and secondary schools, now housed in splendid premises in Bishan, are witness to this.

After her departure there was continuing expansion and devoted service from many who first came to Christian discipleship through the schools. The elder who chaired the committee which organised Katong Presbyterian Church's fortieth anniversary celebrations in 1997 was a schoolboy and member of the Boys' Brigade in the 1950s. Katong Presbyterian Church and its daughter church in Bishan illustrate the vigour and growth of the whole church in Singapore and its commitment to evangelism and expansion as Singapore itself grows. Such churches and the schools are a lasting tribute to those like Monica Sirkett who worked with such singleminded devotion in the early days.

Bernarr and Margaret Atherton *went to Singapore in 1951. As an educational missionary he was headmaster and guided the development of the English-medium Presbyterian Boys' School. In 1958, believing that well-trained local people should take over positions of responsibility, he resigned and returned to the UK, where he continued his career in education.*

On or around February 10th, 1951, my second day in the school, when I was midway through taking my first Assembly, the shutters of the hall in which it was held were closed and a young man came on to the stage and began addressing the Assembly in Chinese. I was baffled. Was it some part of the Assembly I hadn't been told about? So I went over to ask Mr Tan Keng Kang at the piano. He was sitting bolt upright, looking a bit pale, and whispered out of the corner of his mouth, "It's a Communist raid". This was an eventuality I hadn't been trained for, so I had to make up my mind in a split second. What should I do; stay quiet, or resist and encourage others to do the same, or try to jump out of the window to escape and get help. I could now see that there were several intruders, and that they appeared armed as they had something sticking out of their coat pockets. I thought that physical resistance might result in some of the pupils being injured or killed, and that my chances of getting out of a window would be almost zero , so I stayed quiet. One intruder frisked me, saying politely, "Very sorry" as he did so. He asked me for my identity card and I truthfully told him that I didn't have one - I was so newly arrived that it hadn't yet been issued. Fortunately he didn't find my British Passport in my back pocket. About 80 of the pupils' ID cards were torn up, the Red Flag run up on the flag-pole, and the Assembly treated to a Communist harangue. Then they all left on their bicycles. I ran to the 'phone in my office and found the school clerk looking petrified. Before long a Police patrol car arrived and I went with it round the local streets but without seeing anybody we could identify. Later, with some of the pupils, I went to the Central Police Station for an Identity Parade. The Director of Education told me off for failing to resist the raid physically, but my missionary colleagues unanimously and strongly agreed I had done the right thing not to have risked bloodshed.

The reason that some idealistic young people embraced Communism in those days was brought home to me forcibly the same week. I was amazed to discover that nearly six years after the war ended, a number of pupils were still suffering from malnutrition., and the teachers were distributing United Nations Skimmed Milk to them at break-time. I joined in and was horrified to see brown sores on boys' legs. This reinforced my already strong Christian Socialist ideas.

There was a tremendous backlog of educational needs following the war and the closure of schools for a time by the Japanese, compounded by the awful economic conditions which were only slowly being overcome. So my Head Prefect was 21 years old (I was 28!) In many Government Schools the only trained teacher was the Principal; all the others were half the day teaching and the other half at the Teacher Training College. Soon after I arrived the Principal of the TTC 'phoned to tell me that I had to give some lectures at the College. He suggested every afternoon and Saturday mornings but I managed to reduce this to two afternoons and Saturday mornings. I lectured on Education and English Literature. I was not trained for the latter, but was told, "We all have to help as best we can in an emergency."

An emergency it was. By a tremendous effort on the part of Government schools, Church schools and the Training College, the number of pupils on roll in Government schools was increased tenfold in the ten years 1945-1955, while Church schools with their smaller resources increased two and a quarterfold. Then, for the first time, in 1955 we could offer a Primary school place to all Singapore children. For some years, at Secondary level many pupils were over-age. Others had completed their

Chinese Senior Middle School education and wished to have a year with us to get their Cambridge School Certificate also. Others who had narrowly failed wished to re-sit. The pressure on places at Secondary level was intense. In the early days I often had to refuse to take a child when every class of his age group was full (44). Knowing that my refusal meant there was no place anywhere for him, and with his mother crying in my office, was harrowing. Another dimension of the educational needs can be gauged from the fact that the Teacher Training College Principal rang me one day and said, "Atherton, you're a new young chap with fresh ideas. The Colonial Office have just given me £2000 to restart the TTC Library which was destroyed in the war. Make a list of books I should order." At the end of each day, after working flat out, I felt exhausted.

We had to collect school fees and take them weekly to the Bank, initially at Collyer Quay. It was sometimes a rush to get there before the Bank closed, especially when Kallang Road was temporarily closed by aircraft landing or taking off from the old airstrip, Kallang Airport, which crossed it. On one such occasion I was stopped in my speeding by a traffic policeman, who inspected my licence, saw my name, looked at me closely, and then said, "Didn't you lecture to me at the TTC?" I said, "Yes", and he said, "Go off and don't speed again".

One other thing which lay heavily on my mind (I was a Physics graduate) was that there was no Science Laboratory in the school, with the result that the pupils' education was limited and some professions virtually closed to them. It was a challenge to raise a Building Fund and qualify for the Government's dollar-for-dollar grant for approved building and equipment. So like other missionary colleagues I learnt the art of the begging bowl. S$7000 from Tan Lark Sye (a leading Chinese businessman) raised our spirits, and even more a grant from the Synod following the Johore Government's compulsory purchase of the Roseley Estate. On leave in England in 1954 I also collected some money, notably from Mr Gray Buchanan, a leading Presbyterian layman, who had business interests in Singapore, Messrs William Jacks.

At the end of 1954 we took the plunge and drew up plans for the Physics, Chemistry and Biology Labs., Preparation Room, Library and extra classrooms. Robert Tully took responsibility for Biology matters, Hee Ah Ngot for Chemistry, and I for Physics. After tests the Architects said we should have piling foundations which were cheaper than the alternative spread concrete ones. But one day, looking out, I saw the builder was using spread concrete and I wasn't sure we had enough money for that. A 'phone call to the Architects brought the cool response that they had forgotten to tell us of the change which in turn brought a big argument. The building was finally completed but the builder went bankrupt doing it.

Then we three teachers set about listing every necessary item of equipment, obtaining quotations from firms in Sydney, Birmingham and London, and finally ordering the cheapest in each case. Eventually they all arrived and we had the thrill of first seeing things like laboratory sinks and taps being joined up, and then the beakers, chemicals, balances and so on appear. When all was complete the Minister of Education and the Moderator of Synod came to open our new Science building, and we three members of staff had the thrill of each teaching in a lab. we had designed ourselves; that is a privilege few teachers ever enjoy and made up for the hard slog it had all involved. Our enthusiasm was shared by our pupils. The first group to take advantage of the labs. were determined to succeed, and they and we three teachers used to come in on Saturday mornings for classes, which included a sprinkling of girls from Kuo Chuan and St. Hilda's Schools. Starting from scratch, they all passed an O level in a Science subject in one year.

During his training for the Presbyterian ministry **John Henderson** *felt called to serve in the world-wide mission of the Church. He was appointed to work in Singapore and Malaya and served there from 1950 to 1976. In 1962 he was married in Singapore to* **Daphne McCann**, *a Methodist missionary from South India; and their three children, all born in Malaysia had their early education there. On his return to the UK he continued his ministry at Scarborough until retirement.*

My years in Singapore and Malaysia saw major political changes and dramatic social and economic development. When I went there in 1950 the "Emergency" was at its height in both territories, and the British colonial government was struggling to maintain its authority and defeat the communist-inspired guerrilla activities which threatened the economic life of the country. By the time I left in 1976 two independent democracies, Malaysia and Singapore, had proved their abilities for rapid development, socially and economically, and were living at peace both within and beyond their frontiers. So far as the Church I had been appointed to serve was concerned, the Singapore-Malaya Synod of the Chinese Christian Church, as it was called at that time, it had divided into two independent Churches;

both had reverted to denominational names, the Presbyterian Church in Singapore and the Presbyterian Church in Malaya. Within these two churches were now integrated the former, at that time largely expatriate, congregations which had once been part of the Presbyterian Church of England.

Because of the urgency of the times, not least the fact that Tom Gibson, the only serving ministerial missionary in Singapore or Malaya, was due to retire within the year, I was sent out without the usual missionary preparation course at Selly Oak. My "orientation" went alongside my study of the Hokkien (Amoy) dialect of Chinese, spoken by the largest number of Chinese in Singapore. During that time I owed much to a fairly recently arrived minister from Amoy, the Revd Ho Yew Sam. I met him first on a visit to Muar, when, I recall, he taught me the Lord's Prayer in Hokkien. He then moved to a church in Singapore and I joined in his Youth Fellowship. I also went with him to share in home services of his members. At one of these I experienced through him the Chinese virtue of *cheng-li*. During my time at theological college I had begun to smoke, and on this occasion, after the service, I was offered and politely accepted a cigarette from the husband of the lady whose home we were visiting. He was not a church member. The woman evangelist with us was shocked at my action and was about to lead a walk-out of the members. But the minister must have signalled to her and they all sat down again. That was *cheng-li*. It is almost untranslatable, but it means that human relations must be governed by a combination of morality and sensitivity. Thereafter the woman evangelist's attitude to me was always most cordial; and she didn't even know that about that time I gave up smoking because of the lung cancer scare! On many other occasions, and especially in church meetings, I recall some action being commended or recommended as befitting both *cheng* and *li*.

My move to Muar in late 1951 brought me into closer contact with the major public security experiment of the period, the "New Villages". In order to protect the scattered rural population from the jungle based terrorists and at the same time cut off the latter's source of supplies, half a million people were resettled in about 500 New Villages and protected with armed police and barbed wire fences. In many cases they were existing villages but now greatly enlarged. There was also a nightly curfew preventing travel in and out between dusk and dawn. Most of those resettled were Chinese and many of these villages were in Johore where the Synod already had a number of congregations in both towns and villages. My colleague in Muar was Mack Neave, formerly in South Fujian, and he and his Chinese colleagues had already set up the "Muar District Evangelistic Band" which once a month, as a body, visited a nearby town or village to do open-air preaching. As a result, regular services were started in two of the New Villages. In those early days I was in charge of the public address system which the Band had bought, and had to cope with rather uncertain electricity supplies. Sometimes we were able to use the film van of the Malayan Christian Council inside the perimeter fence after dark, alternating preaching with the showing of Christian films. On one occasion, half way through the performance, rifle shots were heard. Terrorists had been found by the police as they tried to enter the village. Our audience immediately fled to their homes, in their haste leaving about a hundred pairs of clogs and slippers on the ground.

As missionaries did elsewhere, Mack Neave had started an English-language service in Muar, attended by Indians and Eurasians as well as Chinese. An Indian evangelist came for a series of meetings in English, and he joined us on one of our film outings to a rubber estate, where, as so often, many of the rubber-tappers were Tamils. So both Chinese and Tamils heard the gospel in their own languages. I also used the film van in five New Villages some distance from Muar. In one of them I asked Daphne to teach Christian choruses to Tamil children as well as Chinese. The former were the faster learners under her tuition.

In my film evangelism work I was blessed with a number of capable young assistants. For two of them I should be grateful to Trinity Theological College in Singapore. During Japanese occupation three missionaries were interned together, Bishop Wilson from the Anglican Church, Bishop Amstutz of the American Methodist Episcopal Church and our own Tom Gibson. Although they had no idea if they would survive detention they discussed in hope the future of the Church in Singapore and Malaya. Robert Greer, minister of Orchard Road Presbyterian Church, also shared in the discussions in which they agreed that their three denominations should unite in the training of a future ministry. As a result of their thinking plans were made and Trinity Theological College was opened in 1948. One of the first Presbyterian graduates came to me at Muar in a college vacation posting and helped by running the projector at several open air film meetings. He was Stephen Tan. During this vacation visit I happened to be taking the Sunday service at one of the two Muar churches so I invited him to conduct the service while I took the sermon. On our way to church a learner driver drove out of a side road striking my off-side fairly and squarely in the middle. My car ended on its side facing the direction from which we had come. We were not injured. The learner driver ran away. I had to wait till the police arrived, but Stephen went on to the church by himself and - satisfactorily - conducted the whole service. His sermon was unscripted and impromptu! After graduation Stephen's first appointment was in one of the central Johore New Villages, with responsibility for two others, and there he organized open air evangelism. Later he was ordained minister at Kluang and after ministry there and in Singapore, was called to be on the staff of Trinity, of which he eventually became principal. Most recently he has been a visiting lecturer at Nanjing and other theological seminaries in China and also helped conduct lay-training courses there.

Another Presbyterian graduate, Chong Kah Geh, also helped me in the film evangelism work. He too began his ministry in Johore New Villages. After serving in Kuala Lumpur and on the staff of Trinity he became the Synod's first overseas missionary. For many years he has been in London working as a chaplain among Chinese students and increasingly among the wider Chinese community.

At that time the Synod was very short of ordained ministers and the majority of them were in Singapore, or in the few Malayan congregations which were financially self-supporting. The Synod made me interim-moderator of five New Village churches as well as three others around and in Muar. Some of these had unordained preachers in charge, so 'interim-moderator' could be interpreted as 'peripatetic celebrant of the sacraments', an unsatisfactory role in some ways but compensated for by my getting to know many congregations, and even more the men and women who served them.

The fellowship enjoyed with our Chinese colleagues was well expressed in the annual church-workers conferences/retreats. For many of them this annual week away from their churches was the nearest thing they had to a holiday and an opportunity to see hitherto unvisited parts of Malaysia. In 1961, with the strains and stresses of the Emergency over, and about the same time as Singapore and Malaysia emerged into separate nationhood, the Synod, inspired by one of its most senior ministers, the Revd Yap Kok Hu, launched the Five Year Doubling Movement. Although the hope and aim was such a dramatic increase in both membership and congregations, the emphasis throughout was on revitalising the church at every level. Each year had a theme and watchword, promoted throughout the church, expressed in a hymn written specially by Pastor Yap, a poster for every household and other materials. Well-known evangelists from Taiwan and elsewhere were invited who both conducted missions at congregational level and played an important role in the church-workers retreats. At the first of these following the beginning of the Doubling Movement the church-workers set an example to the rest of the church by promising personal monthly donations to fund the movement. This was taken up by many members and the money raised helped the opening of new congregations in Penang, Klang, Kuala Lumpur and Ipoh.

Throughout my remaining years in Malaysia I was involved in one way or another with the Five Year Movement, the second five year period which followed, and the continuing emphasis on growth and church extension which is now bearing fruit. It involved taking the film van from Penang in the north to the Pengerang peninsula in the south, serving the churches in Kelantan and Trengganu, prospecting possible extension in Pahang, and continuing some of the work which George Hood had done as FYM general secretary. There have been disappointments but the overall memory is of growth and fellowship in the Gospel.

George and Beth Hood went to China in 1945 and served there till 1950. After the withdrawal of missionaries they served in Malaysia till 1972 when George became East Asia Secretary of the Council for World Mission , followed by five years teaching in the Selly Oak Colleges, until retirement in 1982.

Some periods of service overseas seem full of memories, while for others there is no button for instant recall. One of the most memorable was our first four years in Malaysia. That was partly because of the contrast between it and the previous five years in China. In the Lingdong (Swatow/Hakka) field, like most of my missionary colleagues we had lived in a traditional mission compound, in our case at Chaozhou (Chao-an), one in which my wife, Beth, had played as a child. When we were there, only two buildings housed missionaries, Agnes Richards in one of them, and ourselves in the other. All the other former hospital buildings were used for a Women's School and the re-opened Pue-li Theological College, previously located in Swatow. We all taught in both of them but my main work was in the College, of which our oldest Chinese friend, Anna Ling, was principal.

When we were invited to work in Singapore and Malaya, we were all anxious to escape the 'mission compound syndrome' against which so much criticism had been levelled. We were keen to be close to the work we were doing. Agnes felt called to work in the New Villages, and with her London Missionary Society colleague, Joyce Lovell, formerly in north

China, made Kulai the centre of their work.

We were appointed by the Synod to be based in Johore Bahru, and for me to be the resident interim-moderator of the Holy Light Church, which made me in effect the minister of that congregation. By contrast to the solid church buildings in China, this church was a very simple sixty-year old wooden structure with a corrugated iron roof, set in a three-acre triangle of land, between the prison and the Roman Catholic church. The entrance to this valuable plot had the same appearance as to the rubber estates throughout the country, a two by twelve foot horizontal zinc board, with the name in both Chinese and English, supported by posts on either side and high enough for a lorry to get through. On the church's land there were indeed some old rubber trees, no longer worth tapping, and a much more valuable collection of durian trees close to the house in which we were to live. When ripe the precious durians fall at night, and they fell like bombs on the corrugated iron roof of our upstairs verandah. Beth combined attending to our baby Catherine, and later Douglas, with going out to collect the durians before others came in to steal them; in the morning we took them to the church treasurer to be sold for church funds.

The congregation and office-bearers, one elder and four deacons at that time, had been rather uncertain about having a 'red hair' living among them. No missionary had lived there previously, and their contacts with foreigners were either with the police or other more remote government officials. It was also the height of the 'Emergency' when too close contact with those of the same race as the colonial rulers was not everyone's choice. I learned from Harry Johnston, acting as both Synod and Mission Council secretary, that the Mission's willingness to make the 'manse' more habitable had been something of a 'sweetener', not a very auspicious start to what proved four of the happiest years of our lives.

The two-storey house had plaster-coated brick pillars but the rest was wood; it had been built forty years earlier to house both a preacher and those church members who lived at a distance and needed overnight accommodation when they came to worship. It consisted of three rooms in a row downstairs, opening out of each other, and the same upstairs. But to get upstairs you had to go into a covered yard behind and from there climb up a wooden staircase. One third of the yard was divided off to make a kitchen with an oil-stove for cooking, and further back were two cubicles, one for bathing by throwing water over yourself, and one with a bucket, emptied every day by the night-soil collector. This yard had also served as a rubber smoke-house, its corrugated iron roof was blackened with soot, festooned with cobwebs, and a lurking place for vicious, giant centipedes. But there was a good electricity supply, we had running cold water and a refrigerator, something we had not aspired to in China.

Being effectively full-time minister of a congregation was a different experience from anything we had known in China. Normally I conducted the Chinese service in the morning, but when I was visiting other churches, I had a visiting preacher; the office-bearers, especially our one and only elder, gave great help in both services and home meetings. The congregation's dialects were many, at least five or six, among which the Swatow dialect predominated, but each dialect borrowed words from the others with some Malay also thrown in. In September of that first year, 1952, we began a weekly English-speaking service, the first of several in our Johore churches, and it brought together English-speaking Chinese and Indians, as well as Europeans, from Government, rubber estates and National Service men - the latter a regular group for Sunday supper.

But the most satisfying and memorable times were with the young people. Two wooden classrooms survived from a church school, now closed and one of these was a Youth Fellowship meeting place. The young people provided the choir, the Sunday School teachers, and when special occasions required, the cleaners and decorators of the church building. More than that, they acted as a kind of dynamo which kept energising the determination, already present on our arrival, to build a better church. In this project we were able to enlist the voluntary help of the state architect, a regular attender at the English service and whose wife was its pianist; he designed a lovely church which set a new standard for church building throughout the Synod. And by necessity I learned the skill of the begging bowl, within and beyond the bounds of our congregation, and was repeatedly amazed at Chinese generosity when building churches.

The young people also provided friendship. Rarely did a day pass without two or three of them sharing time and themselves with us. They delighted in our children, taking turns to carry them from the earliest days. They enjoyed improving the church grounds, and in the evening, after the end of their meetings or activities, there was the fun of going down with them to the open air market, to sit around a table and enjoy simple Malaysian Chinese food.

During this time I was also interim-moderator of New Village churches in Kulai, Senai, and the two larger towns of Pontian and Kota Tinggi, a radius of forty miles. Sometimes I stayed overnight for an English service in Pontian. Afternoon services such as those at Pontian and Kulai were not uncommon; it was a time when most people would have liked a snooze but it enabled rubber-tappers who had started work at dawn to attend. My recurrent nightmare was that with my eyes closed I might fall asleep as I was praying.

During those four years all the restrictions imposed by the 'Emergency' were part of daily living. Johore State had more than its fair share of 'incidents'. Although most attacks were directed against the police, the military and the rubber estates, and - so far as I know - no missionaries were attacked, it was always with some feeling of relief that one got past 'black spots', stretches of road where things had happened. My only encounter was with those supposedly 'on our side', namely the Special Branch, who came in the early hours of the morning to search the Youth Fellowship room and took away church magazines sent from China. I had to appear and be interrogated at the Police Station where eventually I was told the magazines, if not subversive were at least 'prejudicial'. A simultaneous raid on our Chinese colleague, the preacher at Senai and Kulai, had been much more threatening for him, his wife, and his large family of small children.

Those four memorable years converted us from looking back to China to looking forward to Malaysia.

In 1961 the Synod decided to embark on a Five Year Movement (FYM) to double the size of the church. We were on furlough at the time, settling our ten and eight year old children into boarding schools, and on our return to Malaysia discovered I had been appointed secretary of the FYM. By this time we were living at Kluang in the centre of Johore state, and were most fortunate to have as friends and colleagues Chen Fu Sheng (Tan Hock Seng) and his wife Su Chun who had come from Taiwan to work in the Synod. He was minister of Kluang and then went on to the staff of Trinity Theological College in Singapore. (In 1969, just as he was completing Ph D studies at New College, Edinburgh he died of a heart attack, one of the saddest events of my life). They were wonderful God-given friends at a time when we needed them most, able to share the deepest feelings and problems as well as daily incidents and gossip, FYM ideas and plans, Taiwanese experience, and to see the situation in Singapore and Malaysia and life in a local congregation through fresh Asian eyes. And all the time there was humour, especially on the several holidays we spent together.

The FYM required a lot of travelling, to the north-east, throughout Johore and Singapore. One year we lived a third of the time in each. During our time in Johore Bahru, Beth had found a need crying out to be met, the spastic children in the Children's Home for whose special needs there was not the qualified staff. With help from some expatriate wives in the Naval Base and the guidance of the Hospital Singhalese paediatrician, and after three years of struggle, a Spastic Association of Johore was established, which qualified for government aid. After 1962, no longer with family responsiblities, Beth usually accompanied me on my travels and soon discovered another need which she could fill, making Christian literature, bibles, books and pictures available to congregations.. Regular visits to the several Christian bookshops in Singapore provided a wide range for sale and any profits were passed on in the form of gifts of books to Youth Fellowships and Sunday Schools.

'I only count the sunny hours' confesses the sundial outside Westminster College where many of us trained. I don't admit quite so much for we had some less than 'sunny hours', mostly related to property disputes, but memories of the sunny ones prevail.

Jim Swanston *was appointed in 1956 to be head of the newly established English School at Kulai, Johore. He and his wife* **Catherine** *served there for eight years, during which time their four children were born. Having overseen the school building programme and its development to Secondary School standard, they returned to the UK in 1964.*

We were awakened early in the morning by a loudspeaker touring the village but we could not understand a word of the several languages being spoken. We had only been in Kulai for a few weeks but fortunately Agnes Richards and Joyce Lovell, our colleagues and former China missionaries with several Chinese dialects between them, were still in the village. We 'phoned them and found that there had been a terrorist raid on the village during the night and that we were now under a total curfew. Soon, friends from Singapore rang asking if Catherine was alright (she was 21 and almost nine months pregnant) as they had newspaper headlines, "Night of Terror in Kulai."

Soon life was back to normal. The new school building was almost ready to use following Agnes' great efforts to raise the money, but meanwhile we still had 120 children in four classrooms in the Hainanese

Pilgrims in Mission   Memories: Singapore and Malaysia

temple. The Hainanese community had had to abandon it because it was outside the perimeter fence, and Agnes had been able to negotiate the temporary use of it.

By January '57 we were in the new building and the floodgates opened. 112 children had to be taken into two classes, and, until we got the proper staffing and equipment, my abiding mental picture is of Mrs Wong with 57 children sitting on mats on the floor being taught English. None of them had English as their mother tongue and there were at least seven languages or dialects, Chinese, Indian and Malay, spoken between them. Six years later they were passing in good numbers the Malayan Secondary Schools Entrance examination on a par with the English 11+ exam.

Within three years we were bursting at the seams in spite of having three schools in the one building . The morning school ran from 6.45 a.m. to 12.30 p.m.; then there was a quarter of an hour's chaos as 200 morning school pupils went home and afternoon pupils came in to start from 12.45 p.m. to 6.30 p.m. followed by an evening school from 7 p.m. to 9 p.m. School building was in the programme again. I'm not even capable of selling a raffle ticket so I was grateful for the help of our church members, and I can still picture Mr Chai Kim Piow going round the village asking each shop and house for a donation with myself standing mute and embarrassed behind. The building, although not as fine as that organised by Agnes, was erected quickly and is still there.

So great was the desire to learn English that in 1961 a system was put into operation to enable all pupils with grades A & B in the entrance examination to transfer to English-speaking Secondary School even though their six years Primary had been in Chinese, Malay or Tamil. They were given a year in the 'Remove' class to learn English. That meant a further rapid increase in numbers so hasty negotiations within the community resulted in our renewed tenancy of the old temple classrooms. However, by this time we had lost our 'Black Area' terrorist status and the fence was down so we shared the building. The temple area was beyond the classrooms. One morning, on asking the meaning of some particularly noisy activity coming from it, I was told they were asking the gods which horse was going to win in the Singapore races.

Religious teaching was restricted by law. So pre-school worship was held, for those wanting it, in the fifteen minutes before school opened, morning and afternoon. However, there were youth activities based on the church. Joyce and Agnes had a flourishing Girls Life Brigade and later we started a Boys Brigade. The latter did not last long because Mr Muthiah and I were heavily engaged in the expanding school and other leaders were not around to help. Long after we left Malaysia we found that some of our senior boys had started it up again and it was flourishing. A later memory from our visit in 1988 was of a march past and display from strong GLB and BB Companies complete with band. Sunday School and Bible Study were mainly on Saturday because the main services in the church were Chinese speaking and held there on Sunday. At first the English medium Sunday School was run by missionaries and a few English-speaking Christians already in the village, but by 1964 some of the older pupils were taking classes.

English was undoubtedly popular as a medium for instruction but for normal communications in the village it was barely used. Contacts in the State Education Department in Johore Bahru were still in English but Malayanisation was coming in fast, and the 'National Language' becoming the norm and a compulsory subject on the curriculum. Relying on English seemed to give a hint of the old colonialism. In our time the Synod had no English-speaking Chinese ministers in Malaysia and only one in Singapore. For communion services, if George Hood, Dick Shad or Bob Elder, successively based in Johore Bahru, were not available, we had to invite John Henderson, 90 miles away in Muar, to officiate.

In 1988 when we visited Kulai we had a wonderful welcome. Former pupils, Nallu and Lui, were our minders and they took us to the school; no longer 'The English School' but 'Sekolah Rendah' with Malay as the medium for teaching and a Haji as head of the afternoon school. They also took us to the government Secondary School with about 3000 pupils where they were school secretaries.

Had it all been a waste of effort? I hope not. That group which welcomed us in '88 contained many of our Sunday School and BB members. Both GLB and BB flourish and an Indian pastor is in charge of the English-speaking congregation. Soon Moy, another former pupil, herself now head teacher in a big school in Mersing, is an active member of the old church. And finally, I wonder what would have happened to education in Kulai if Agnes Richards, as an adjunct to her Chinese-speaking work, had not started an English Kindergarten in 1952 in the back room of the church there; because it grew until a secondary section split off from the primary to become the biggest school in the country in 1970.

Janet (Dukes) Lovett-Hargis served in the north-east of Malaya, Trengganu state, from 1958 to 1962. When family reasons prevented her return after furlough, she studied and obtained a degree in Chinese at London University, but was then prevented from returning by new Malaysian government restrictions on missionary service.

I arrived in Malaysia in the autumn of 1958. In those days, the 'Home Church' sent a person abroad and the 'Receiving Church' was given the responsibility of deciding where they should work. The Chinese Christian Church leaders asked me to go to work in Trengganu State, on the North East coast. I was the first British missionary to be stationed there, but I had a colleague, Revd Tan Hau Chan, who with his wife and three children had come as missionaries from Taiwan.

First I had to learn the languages, so I joined Nan Lindsay in Kota Bharu for the monsoon season, studied Malay and learnt from Nan how to understand the local culture and get acquainted with the ways of the local Church. Then, after a year in Kuala Lumpur at the Government Officers Language School, learning Mandarin Chinese, I returned to Trengganu.

My first memory on arrival was going to the house which the local church had prepared. It was a shop which had been a grain store. I got a dog very soon and she proved brilliant at catching the rats that I knocked down with my broom! I also taught the dog to rush into the outside toilet, and chase out whatever was sleeping there before I went in. This led to a near disaster when Celia Downward came to stay and I forgot to tell her about it. She had to go out in the night and nearly had a heart attack when the dog leapt into the outhouse before her. Later the WMA helped us build a house beside the new church for the Tan family and myself.

Living at close quarters with the Tan family and so often eating together I learnt a lot. Going to market with Chun Uan (Mrs Tan) was a lesson in bargaining and when we returned she showed me how to cook. Birthdays are a very special memory, for on these occasions we had a tradition of taking each other out, which meant going to the beach and providing satay. Nowhere else and at no other time have I ever tasted such delicious satay.

As the Tan family spoke the dialect of the older Chinese and I had learnt Mandarin, the language of the younger, we arranged that I would have a Sunday School and Youth group to look after, taking occasional services which were translated by an elder. I also found an English speaking family and together we built up an English language service in the town.

Once a month I went down the coast to help the churches in the rest of the state, The coast road passed through beautiful scenery and also crossed two wide rivers. There were no bridges at that time. A raft was tied to a motor boat and brought to a slope. To get the car onto the raft you had to drive onto two planks. There was much gesticulating by the ferryman, but at least I never once drove the mission car into the river.

The journey took most of the morning but waiting for the ferry, there was always someone to talk to and stalls for a snack. I remember a particularly delicious fish soup for a few cents. I had some favourite stopping places and usually took a walk at 'Janet's Bay'.

Halfway along the road I stopped at Dungun. The church met in a house and after a cool wash of the feet, I would lead worship and then go to various houses to visit and to pray, especially if someone was ill. There was always a language problem here. Once, I was taken to visit a woman who was very ill indeed. Using Mandarin, I prayed for comfort, peace and a good rest. As I said Amen, the elders with me said to the woman, "The Teacher has prayed for you, you are well now", and they got her out of bed and she walked about the house. I really began to pray then......that she would not immediately drop down dead! However, there she was at the next service.

When I arrived in Kemaman, my final destination, the preacher there and I would drive round the town, calling at all the members' houses, and saying, "The Teacher has come, worship is at 6.00 p.m. Come". As the time passed he would simply shout from the car. I think this practice went back to the time when travel was more difficult and the preacher might not arrive at all, or perhaps it was the pleasure of riding about in the mission car. In Kemaman we also started Bible study and worship for the few English-speaking Asians in the town. One of the best letters I received after I returned to England was from this group saying, "We are still going to church even though you are not here". Another piece of outreach was at Kuala Kemaman, at the mouth of the river, reached by launch. Here our meeting place was in the house of a family who dried fish for a living, and sold it throughout the country. Both the house and the platform on which the fish were dried, were built over the river and the smell of the fish was all pervasive. On my monthly visits, armed with flannelgraphs, other visual aids and much drama, (language again being a problem), the crowd of children grew at a great rate. I was thinking that it must be something to do with my excellent preaching when I discovered that the local preacher had been bringing an ever bigger bag of sweets each time we came.

At the Chinese services in Kemaman, I preached in Mandarin and Mr See translated into the Amoy dialect. Laboriously I had prepared about five minutes worth of sermon, but it always took about twenty to be translated. I heard a phrase often enough for me to learn it. It turned out he was saying, "What she said was..... but what she meant was......" At last, after two years or so, the time taken in translation began to match the time I spoke.

I stayed down the coast for three or four days at a time, visiting, leading Bible studies and worship, before returning home. Once I risked going late and the monsoon started with the result that I had to be pushed across a bridge by friendly and highly amused Malay villagers. The river was flowing over the bridge and only they knew where it was.

There was not much to do for relaxation in Kuala Trengganu apart from walking on the beach with my dog. But sometimes other missionary colleagues would come to stay and we would take an overnight trip to see the great leatherback turtles lay their eggs, sleeping alongside them on the beach. When I needed to have a longer break I travelled north into Kelantan state where Frank and Flo Buxton, LMS colleagues, were based. We had a ritual; when I arrived I had a bath and a long drink and then they would listen to me for two hours. After that I was able to listen to them! I don't think it was really as bad as that but that is definitely the memory. It must have been something to do with hardly having spoken any English for weeks!

Sadly I had to stop work as a missionary for family reasons in 1962. When I was able to return the Malaysian Government refused to give me a visa. I was very disappointed as I had enjoyed the place, the work and especially the friends in the Chinese speaking and English speaking communities.

After ministries at West Stanley and Richmond, **David and Mary Marsden** *served in Singapore and Malaysia from 1967 to 1973. On their return to the UK they served in Redditch Ecumenical Centre and in the South Leeds team until retirement in 1994.*

The memory of our first arrival in Singapore on a sunny Sunday morning at the beginning of January 1967 will live with us forever. Before we could attract the attention of missionary colleagues awaiting us on the quay, we were greeted by a party of Singaporean church folk who had already boarded the ship and welcomed us right there on the deck with a bunch of home grown orchids. From that moment the story of our experience has been one of the embracing love of Christian fellowship which makes us feel Singapore to be home as much as anywhere we have lived in this country.

The ensuing days and weeks were a discovery of the differences in exercising the universal task of ministry in a new context. The work was a continuation of preaching the Gospel, teaching and encouraging in the Christian way, pastoring folk in the chances and changes of life - all of it our calling in England over the previous dozen years. We had come to Singapore as part of the Presbyterian Church of England's response to the appeal of what was then still called the Malaysia Synod of the Chinese Christian Church to assist in the development of the church's work in English. Not only did our ears have to become attuned to the Singaporean English of the young folk of Katong, but we also had to understand that much of our vocabulary seemed quaint to them. We had to think out anew how to say things in our mother tongue. Chaplaincy in the Church's Schools at the flag-raising ceremony and pledge of loyalty repeated every morning drew us into the process of multi-racial, multi-cultural and multi-religious nation building. Suddenly to be almost the oldest person on the Session took some adjustment. Back in England we had grown up with the understanding that the young churches overseas were far ahead of the British churches in ecumenical awareness and development. We were soon to learn that the dream from afar hardly accorded with the reality in Singapore at least. A new learning process ensued about the causes of Christian division and the influences that kept groups separate from one another. We learned all over again that there were nuances to the established labels of evangelical and liberal and even fundamentalist that we had not encountered before.

In the early years of our time in Singapore, Presbytery and Synod meetings were conducted wholly in Hokkien(Amoy dialect) and Teochew (Swatow dialect). Most of our young church members came from homes where these dialects were spoken daily but very few of them were literate in, or even sufficiently fluent in them, to be able to participate in their scholarly and churchly use. Meetings of Presbytery and Synod lasted longer even than those I had been used to in England, sometimes late into the night. I look back with great gratitude to Miss Wu Shui Hsia and Mrs Goh Hee Peck who, tired after a day's work, struggled to translate for me to keep me in the picture of what was going on. Those meetings were lessons in the priorities of another culture. When the congregations of the former Presbytery of Malaya of the Presbyterian Church of England united with the Chinese churches, translation equipment was provided but this in its turn laid a burden on senior missionary colleagues who had to become participants and interpreters at the same time!

In the first years the task of helping the Chinese churches in Johore state to develop their related English-speaking congregations took me each Sunday northwards across the causeway into peninsular Malaya, involving a return journey driving up to a couple of hundred miles. Morning services, often in two locations, in Singapore, were followed by an afternoon driving to conduct evening services in parts of Johore State, with a late night return to be in position in Singapore for seven o'clock flag-raising at Presbyterian Boys' School next morning. In Singapore also the call for new English services seemed to be erupting everywhere. Returning thirty years after our first arrival in Singapore we have seen the harvest of those new beginnings: established congregations in substantial buildings, standing on their own feet, exercising a ministry stretching out into their neighbourhoods, rearing their own daughter churches and mission enterprises, sometimes reaching beyond their own countries, all this being led and pastored by the youth who were drawn to the faith and been nurtured in the Bible Classes and Youth Fellowships of the sixties and seventies.

As time went on we were joined by other colleagues who came specifically for the English work, from our own Presbyterian Church of England, and also from New Zealand and the USA. Here new friendships were formed, some of which we have managed to maintain over the years since. Their coming meant less driving into peninsular Malaya. At the same time, however, when George and Beth Hood became based in London I was drawn more closely into the Synod administration. Noah Chen was then Synod Clerk and the two of us used to sit across the desk in his home, polishing his English version of his minutes, originally written in Chinese, into a shape to be distributed along with all sorts of other notices and communications which needed to reach the English speaking groups as well as the Chinese speaking. Looking back over these days I realise how much of our time was used in nurturing young people in discipleship as well as in evangelistic programmes. The Church Camps and Retreats that we still hear happening today had their beginning in these wonderful years. Coffee House Evangelism and a Sunday evening outreach, TNT (Teens and Twenties) and the guitar bands which gifted and enthusiastic young folk assembled all stand out in memory.

When the Presbyterian Church of England listed its missionaries, it appended an asterisk to the names of those who were married. Mary lived out the mission of that asterisk, not only as wife and mother, but also in keeping open house to facilitate the coming and going of missionary colleagues pursuing their work on both sides of the Causeway between Singapore and Malaysia, and in providing hospitality for the world church leaders and eminent theologians who passed through South East Asia. In addition her mathematical skills were put to use auditing the accounts of the maternity home at Kulai and the Mission Council. She engaged in her own right in fellowship with members of the national church in the work of the YWCA, the Fellowship of the Least Coin and the World Day of Prayer movement.

We took to Singapore a young family. We returned from Singapore with three young people whose lives had been shaped by their experiences with a vision and attitude to the world which did not make it easy for them to settle back into contemporary educational establishments in Britain. They had been isolated from the turmoil that hit the youth scene in the late sixties in Europe. But experiences in Singapore helped form in them a commitment to Christ's Church in one world. There have remained with all of us enduring friendships in which we have shared experiences which have shaped our ministry ever since.

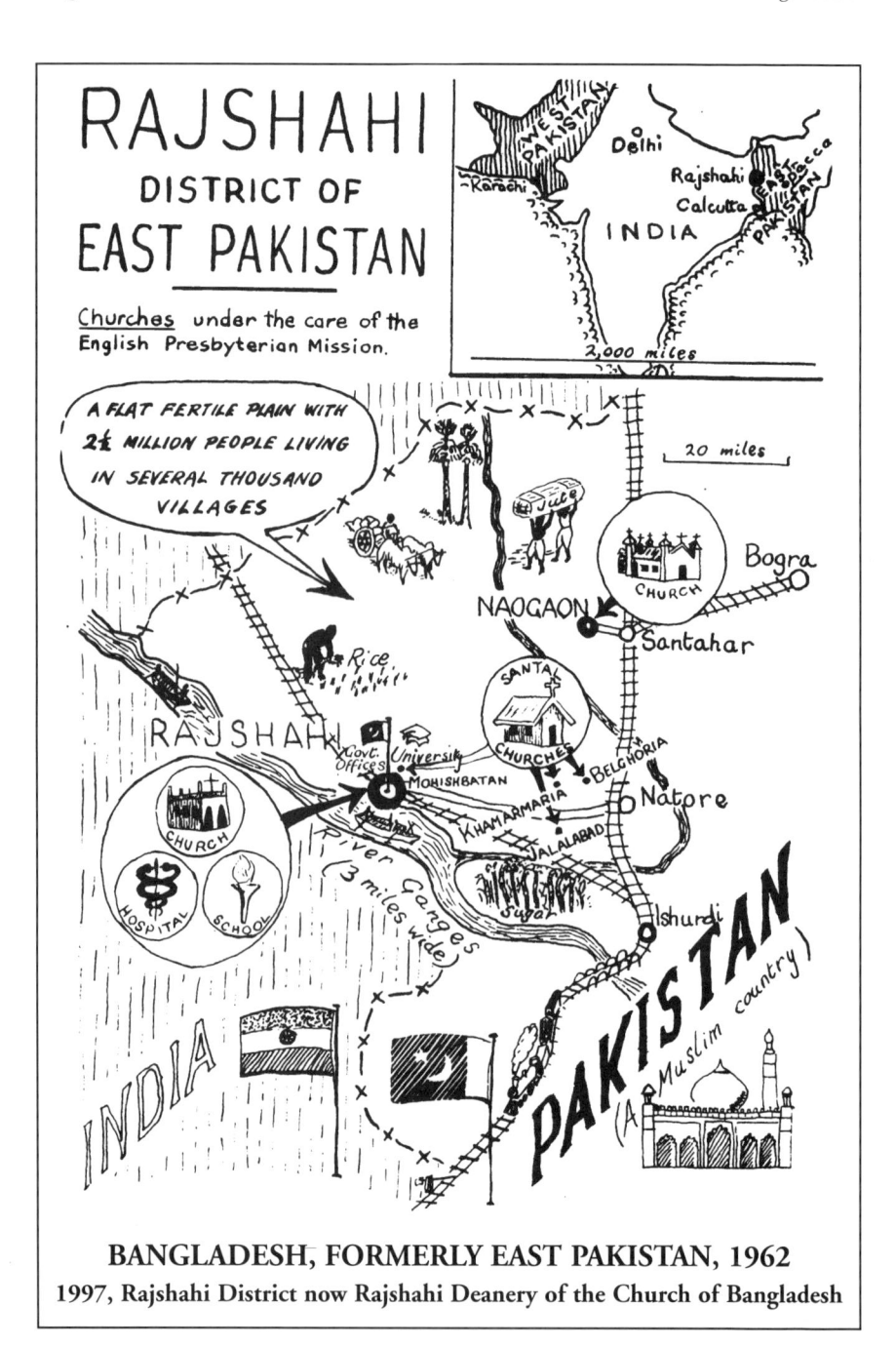

RAJSHAHI
DISTRICT OF
EAST PAKISTAN

Churches under the care of the English Presbyterian Mission.

A FLAT FERTILE PLAIN WITH 2½ MILLION PEOPLE LIVING IN SEVERAL THOUSAND VILLAGES

20 miles

2,000 miles

Delhi
Karachi
WEST PAKISTAN
Rajshahi
Calcutta
Dacca
INDIA

Bogra
NAOGAON
Santahar
Rice
SANTAL
CHURCH
RAJSHAHI
Govt. Offices
University
MOHISHBATAN
CHURCHES
BELGHORIA
KHAMARMARIA
Natore
CHURCH
HOSPITAL
SCHOOL
JALALABAD
River Ganges (3 miles wide)
sugar
Ishurdi
INDIA
PAKISTAN (A Muslim country)

BANGLADESH, FORMERLY EAST PAKISTAN, 1962
1997, Rajshahi District now Rajshahi Deanery of the Church of Bangladesh

MEMORIES: EAST PAKISTAN/BANGLADESH

Alan and Margaret Macleod served in Rajshahi and Naogaon from 1936 to 1955. In that year they returned to the UK for Alan to become OT Professor and later Principal of Westminster College, Cambridge. **Margaret** *has written the following memories of their time overseas.*

In our early years Bengal was still part of the 'Raj' and tradition and social custom held the British ex-pats in a firm grip. In 1939 we moved from Rajshahi to Naogaon where no other foreigners lived. Then came the war and that broke tradition and custom everywhere. Army personnel (British and American) were stationed at nearby Santahar - a railway junction. Great numbers of troops passed through on their way to the Burma front. We saw many of them and entertained them in our home. There, and in many railway journeys our children were a centre of attraction. Out came photos of the men's own children back home and all their homesickness was for a moment relieved in the presence of our young ones.

As a family we visited outlying villages in a country boat through growing rice which was flooded to 10 or 12 feet deep - special rice which managed to keep growing above the flood water. The rice parted with a swishing sound as we moved through it, and rose upright again when we passed. At harvest time this long-stalked rice caused many village quarrels because the very long stalks floated over field borders and ownership of the crop was always in doubt.

Teaching and praying in a village home was watched and listened to by other villagers who crowded into the small courtyard. Whether they were drawn by the compelling nature of the teaching or the sight of strange 'white' faces is open to conjecture. "What then? Only that in every way — Christ is proclaimed; and in that I rejoice."

After a prolonged furlough in England (during which Alan had been writing up the account of the Rajshahi mission for Edward Band's book, *Working His Purpose Out*), we sailed for India in a troopship from Liverpool with our two children - Robin age seven, and Christine age three years. Two days and a night on the train from Bombay, and twelve hours more from Calcutta northward landed us at Santahar station - two miles from the Naogaon mission house. We were met at the station by members of the Christian community and many more were on the steps of the house when we drove up on the two-wheeled tum-tum, the children shouting and singing in their excitement at 'coming home'.

It was September when we arrived, Pakistan having come into existence in mid-August 1947. Many of the local folk had become self-consciously Pakistani and among Muslims from neighbouring villages who had joined the welcoming party were young men wearing the red 'fez' and with well-developed beards! On our first Sunday, after the service in the small roadside church we were accosted by a belligerent bearded young man who wanted to know why there was not a Pakistani flag flying from our mission. Apart from having to cross the border-post midway from Calcutta these were the first and early signs of a changed country. Some time later in Rajshahi we noticed that it was the Mission expatriate staff who tried to encourage ordinary people to develop a pride in their country!

After the first few days we managed to settle down to normal routine. We were on our own and 65 miles from the other members of the E.P.Mission staff in Rajshahi. In Naogaon we had a mission dispensary with Pratul Barhoi in charge. He later became an ordained minister of the United Church of North India after years of tuition from Alan.

A vital part of our daily life and of our work was the visit of local Muslims who came to our house to talk with Alan, sometimes a group would be on our verandah - talking, questioning, arguing about the presence of Christians in their midst, and the 'mistaken beliefs' we held. I remember the loudness of the village voices, and I used to think a pitched battle was about to begin. Many of our visitors could not read and certainly did not know Arabic but they could quote from the Quran in support of their arguments. Sometimes they would bring along a village maulvi or priest to add weight to their words. Many came with their personal problems, quarrels with neighbours, disputes over land boundaries, village wells. Divorced wives and widows came for advice and help when they had nowhere to go and no one they could turn to for help.

We had a spell away from home at the Henry Martyn School of Islamics so that Alan could continue his study of Islamics and Arabic. This meant a train journey of about 2000 miles to Aligarh in Uttar Pradesh. It is difficult to remember now those long hot and dusty journeys with two young children. What did we do? All I remember now is watching the changing scenery after leaving the green-ness of Bengal, and pointing out various birds to the children. We saw many different fishing eagle and one saurus crane and many other birds not seen before. While Alan studied, the children's lessons continued along with games and walks. There were no other children around as the Henry Martyn School was near neither village nor town.

Back in Bengal, visiting and staying for brief periods in Santal villages we found the presence of our children drew us closer to our Santal families. Meanwhile Alan was much involved in the new translation of the Bengali Bible and often away from home, taking part with others in translation committees drawn from several missions throughout Bengal. During this time he was also asked to take on the annual April to June Language School for new missionaries in Darjeeling, so each year we set up house there. We enjoyed the contact with young enthusiastic mission workers from many denominations, and the beauty and grandeur of the mountain scenery (the snow peaks of the Kanchenjunga range appearing from time to time) compensated for the rain, and rain and more rain at that time of the year. Landslides, carrying away parts of the only road down to the plains were common. One year they delayed our departure, and when we did go we had to leave our taxi at one level, walk up roped hillsides where the road had disappeared, rejoin the road several hundred feet below and arrange fresh transport from there. Childhood is wonderful and all this was accepted as normal living!

My second son had died of gastro-enteritis as a strong healthy baby of eight months. Memories flood back of that time. We were part of a large missionary community on hot-weather leave in Kashmir and Alan had been booked to take the church service. On the Sunday following the baby's death Alan spoke on the text, 'All things work together for good to them that love God'. That was a hard time.

My third son was born in Kalimpong in 1949. So with an infant to look after and the children to teach my time was quite well filled. I had help from the Parents National Educational Union (PNEU) who supplied books and materials and guidance, and set timetables and examinations for the children according to their age. I continued teaching them daily till our return to England on furlough in August 1951 when they both entered boarding schools for missionaries' children in Kent..

It is easy to write the bare outline details of that time. But no one who has not lived through such abandonment of beloved children can possibly know the anguish that such a decision caused. We knew the children would be in safe hands. We knew our parents were able and willing to supply them with loving care; but the parting was not just an emotional wound to our deepest feelings, it felt like a physical tearing apart. We said goodbye to our boy and girl in a matter-of-fact kind of way but I spent the 150 mile journey to our port of embarkation in silence and with tears streaming down my face. I explained to the children and later I wrote to them from Bengal that we believed God meant us to continue our work together ....and all the other things one says in explaining, but in fact trying to make peace within ourselves. I know we were not alone. I also believe that we were almost the last generation to have to face such a heart-breaking problem. The day dawned, too late for us, when wives were enabled to travel to the home country to be with children at short intervals, and children joined parents during the longer school holidays. God be praised!!

Bryan Dawson trained for the Presbyterian ministry and following a short term at Eastham, he and his wife **Margaret** *served in East Pakistan from 1947 to 1961. On their return to the UK he continued his ministry at Newbiggin, as a Home Secretary for Christian Aid, at Putney, Gloucester, and the Forest of Dean.*

Margaret writes

Memories of East Pakistan (as it was then, now Bangladesh) are coloured, perhaps I should say darkened, by poverty and hunger. 1956 was a year of near famine and the World Council of Churches Inter-Church Aid appealed to the churches for aid. The churches of New Zealand with government aid sent tons of dried milk in huge barrels to each mission in the country. When some of these barrels arrived Bryan said to me, "Over to you" - or words to that effect.

How to cope? I knew that if dried milk was handed out it would only be sold for a few annas and the children would lose out, as usual. I decided that the best way was to mix up the powder and ask mothers with children to come along with bottles or bowls and drink it on the spot. The first day about 20 came - a fixed time had been set - but they were early. Next day there were over 100 and in a very short while - 3000. They came one or two hours early and sat quietly in a huge ring waiting for the delivery time. Our water boy entered into the spirit and ran to and fro filling huge kerosene tins with well water, and we all mixed with a will and poured out milk in record time. The bonanza lasted about six weeks. We had to announce sorrowfully, that there was only a little milk left and only nursing mothers need come. It was almost a miracle - next day only the nursing mothers came and received milk for about a month - then the end of milk.

Weeks later the compound was invaded by a horde of children! The milk is coming! The milk is coming! And sure enough two bullock carts, loaded with barrels were making the two mile journey from the station to the mission house and the routine began again.

We only had difficulties once. With one assignment of milk we received a lot of cooking oil. We told the women to bring bottles the next day to receive oil. Oil is precious and expensive. Next day, instead of the well-behaved crowd of mothers and children, we were invaded by youth and men who swarmed around us in their hundreds (I don't think I am exaggerating). Bryan, coming out of the house was alarmed by the rowdy mob and dealt with it promptly. He got on his motor-bike and herded the youth as a sheep-dog herds a flock of sheep, and when they were safely driven out of the gate, peace was restored and milk and oil distributed.

Bryan writes:

The church building in one of the newly Christian Santal villages in East Pakistan was a simple structure consisting of a raised floor of dried mud with walls of bamboo lattice plastered with mud. It held no furniture and in place of a communion table was an earthen altar, a three-foot cube of dried mud. More down to earth you simply couldn't get. I squatted, one Sunday morning, among the congregation of a dozen or so adults and as many children, cross-legged on the mats of plaited bamboo skin covering the floor. The recently appointed Preacher/Teacher was conducting the simple service. I had picked up the merest smattering of Santali - Bengali being the means of ordinary communication - and my mind was free to wander during the brief sermon. It wandered very far! - from that mud hut to every kind of building around the world in which Christians were at worship, even to the great cathedrals with their long histories and seemingly unquestionable futures. What would become of this hut and its tiny congregation of some of the world's poorest and most deprived, seemingly lost in the teeming population of that non-Christian land? Would it survive? Would this fruit of missionary endeavour, reaching out from my faraway home church, flourish in time to come or wither under all the threatening influences around? A hymn began, the voices rising and swelling to blend with remembered fervour in my home church and imagined exaltation in cathedral choirs We were part of the World Church!. The reality of faith in this group so newly awakened to the joy of the gospel of Christ, so brave in their commitment to him and his church, lifted me up and restored my spirit; to rejoice with them and all the host of faithful souls past, present and to come.

Margaret's description of using the gifts of the World Council of Churches in famine relief relates to the mission compound in Rajshahi itself. I remember vividly the ways in which our local congregations out in the District of Naogaon and the Santal villages rose to the occasion and displayed the greatest responsibility in using supplies of relief goods. Themselves under the same famine threat they used supplies quite selflessly to help as far as possible all in their areas, Christian and non-Christian alike. The Santals, most of all under threat of hunger, sometimes tramping many miles to gather wild roots which only they could eat, carefully divided all the relief that came to them into three parts, and gave one part each to neighbouring Muslim and Hindu villages. When I returned to the UK, perforce, in the early sixties, those experiences had prepared me to respond to a call from Christian Aid, this country's wing of the World Church's Aid programme, to serve for a while with them in this country.

Ian and Molly Patrick served in the Rajshahi Hospital from 1948 to 1958. During that time Ian reorganised and developed the previous two small hospitals and Westminster Hostel into a single hospital. On medical grounds he resigned in 1958, returned to the UK and continued in his profession in Scotland.

One of the greatest problems we had in Rajshahi was Partition. East Pakistan, in which Rajshahi is located, was very poor, an agricultural area which had its natural links with Calcutta through the north-south railway system which followed the course of the rivers of the Ganges-Brahmaputra delta river system.

At partition in 1947, the border with India lay between us and Calcutta. After the UK devaluation of sterling in 1949, India followed the UK and the exchange rate remained the same as before between the rupee and the pound.

Pakistan did not devalue its rupee which meant we received one-third less rupees to the pound than before and all our hospital building programme and day-to-day expenditure depending on money from the UK was cut severely. Also travel to and from Calcutta became more difficult. Direct exchange of Pakistan rupees for Indian was forbidden and one person was only allowed 50 rupees of each currency to be taken across the border. An account had to be set up with the help of another missionary society so that essential supplies not available in Pakistan could be obtained. Customs checks at the border took one and a half hours on each side and medical supplies were not allowed to be carried from India to Pakistan. We had to smuggle items such as suture material for operations, penicillin injections, cotton wool and bandages over the border in our luggage or ladies' handbags. On one occasion a supply of cotton wool was discovered in my bedding roll and confiscated.

We had to improvise. Our precious tubes of catgut were only used for internal suturing. All other layers were stitched with black cotton bought from the local market. We made our own plaster of paris bandages using loose plaster bought locally. We had electricity but no water on tap. All water was carried from a street hydrant by a water carrier. Electricity was too expensive to use to sterilise instruments so we used kerosene. About 1955, when funds became available, we had piped water laid on.

From about 1952, British drug firms opened in Chittagong and Dacca and we were able to get modern anti-malarial drugs and sulpha-group tablets as well as a good range of other supplies.

Two case histories of patients stick in my memory, although I can recall many interesting stories.

In 1954 there was a severe epidemic of smallpox in Rajshahi district. The local Public Health Department carried out mass vaccination in the district while we ensured all our staff and patients were vaccinated or re-vaccinated.

One day a young sailor from one of the river boats which moored along the jetties on the nearby River Padma, was brought in with a "P.U.O." - an undiagnosed fever. 24 hours later, my Bengali colleague, Dr Malakar, diagnosed smallpox. The man was immediately transferred to our isolation room and my wife who is a trained nurse was then the only person allowed to attend him. At the end of a fortnight, that young man's body was so covered with blisters that a pinhead could not be put on an unaffected area. Every orifice - eyes, nose, mouth, was affected and it was with great relief that he passed away at the end of the fortnight.

By 1972 smallpox had been eradicated from the world. That, to me, is the single most important advance in medicine of the last 50 years.

On another occasion, a local farmer fell off the top of a tree. As he fell, a large branch penetrated his chest, transfixing him till he was cut down. When he arrived at the hospital having travelled several miles by bullock-cart, we found that the branch had entered the right side of the chest, passed across to the left side and was pushing out the skin of the chest wall. He was conscious and, of course, in severe pain.

He was taken into our operating theatre. Our anaesthetic consisted of chloroform or ether given by Dr Malakar by open mask. Fortunately, the branch had not damaged any vital organs, passing behind the heart and lungs and in front of the main blood vessel, the aorta. We were able to extract the branch without damaging these vital organs, and then closed the chest wound round a large catheter which we then used to give continuous irrigation with Eusol, a weak antiseptic to try to clean the chest cavity. After about a fortnight we were able to remove the catheter and after a further week he was able to go home and carry on working.

People in rural areas of Bengal are very tough and seem to have a natural resistance to many illnesses.

There are two main types of malaria in Bengal - benign tertian and malignant tertian. Benign is to a Bengali what a bad cold is here - they get over it after a few days with a bottle of quinine mixture.

Malignant tertian is entirely different and can be fatal - some patients go into a coma and die. We developed a technique of giving a dose of adrenalin which constricts the blood-vessels in the peripheral circulation, driving the parasites into the larger blood-vessels, then giving a dose of quinine intravenously. Patients recovered quickly and survived.

Maternity work, however, was our most important field, as there were no women doctors locally and Bengali male doctors were not allowed to examine women. As long as I had a chaperone and the lady covered her face, I was allowed to examine and to operate. Many required Caesarian section for delayed labour. Retained placenta was a common complication of outside deliveries by village midwives.

The hospital gained a high reputation for Christian care. We were able to hold short morning prayer sessions in the wards and to hand out copies of Mark's Gospel and other Christian literature, though open evangelism is prohibited in a Muslim country.

We left Rajshahi in 1958 due to ill-health. The hospital continued to grow under Dr Malakar and his wife Mina who was also a doctor. Funds were raised internationally due to our co-operation with the Lutheran Church locally in our work among the Santal people.

During the war between East and West Pakistan in 1971 which resulted in the birth of Bangladesh, the hospital had to close because fighting raged around Rajshahi. After the war, staff returned to find the hospital intact. The local people realised it had no connection with any government, so they returned gratefully to it for treatment.

Today, the hospital is under Bengali management, has grown from 40 beds to 150 with a recognised nursing school.

Joan (Hope) Paton went to East Pakistan (now Bangladesh) in 1950 to work in the Rajshahi Hospital and served there till 1965. On her return to the UK she married the Revd Percy Paton and shared in his ministry at Seacombe, Embleton and North Sunderland/Seahouses.

Travel and climate, sudden emergencies and almost continual staff shortages, making do with such resources as we had, these are some of my memories.

They began with the first journey out, following the usual route of that time, by sea to Bombay, nearly 1000 miles across India by train to Calcutta, and another 160 miles from there to Rajshahi. There were three lots of customs formalities, in Bombay and on each side of the India-East Pakistan border. I had got to know people on the ship but once ashore in Bombay I was on my own, except for a Shipping Agent. I was alone, but at the same time mesmerised by the sheer mass of humanity and the perpetual noise. Non-stop noise, on the pier, in the Customs Shed, and then at Victoria Station, where I boarded the train for Calcutta, the best part of three days and two nights away. Colleagues met me there for the last lap; at that time the only delay was passing through Customs, but as the years went on, all this changed and everyone was required to have both passports and visas checked. That meant the 160 miles usually took about 18 hours; on one epic journey it took me 31 hours. Journey's end at Rajshahi was something of an anti-climax; no sign of anyone waiting for us at the railway station, and only a seemingly endless journey from there to the mission compound in a box on wheels, pulled by a miserable looking horse whose ribs could be counted. It was late at night and everyone had gone to bed. One of those who had escorted me from Calcutta had sent a card to say we were coming but forgotten to name the day.

In the years that followed I travelled by cycle, cycle rickshaw, pony carts, bullock carts, buses, trains, river boats and planes - each with their own vivid memories. The local buses were miracles of motion but eventually one accepted the miraculous as the norm; of the collection of wires which hung down from where the dashboard should have been, two tied together produced the ignition, and two wound round the steering wheel sounded the horn. If the engine kept jumping out of gear, the gear was wedged with a piece of bamboo. Once a driver asked if anyone had a match so he could go underneath to see what was causing the knocking noise. I handed out my torch - thought it was safer!

But there were other sides to travel. I remember the kindness of the guards on trains when I was boarding in the middle of the night. If there was no empty compartment they would go the full length of the train checking passengers in compartments until they found one with whom they knew I would be safe. There was the fascination of thousands of insects whirling round the station lights. The rail journey to Dhaka was about 17 hours and included one and a half hours by steamer across a branch of the Brahmaputra. I remember lovely night crossings with moonlight and brilliant stars, and coming back in the cool of early morning and the river sparkling. All the time a man stood calling the depth of the water as there were so many sandbanks. Later there was a plane service to Dhaka from Ishurdi (about two hours by rail from Rajshahi); the plane took only 40 minutes to Dhaka and the fare was the same as second class on the train.

As for the weather, for a large part of the year it was either too hot and dry or too wet and humid. In the awful monsoon months, from mid-June to October, it could rain for days on end and then the sun came out. It was like living in a Turkish Bath, with temperatures mainly in the mid-eighties but the humidity 100%. Air letters stuck together and had to be ironed to unstick them. Everything, even carbon paper and the ink pad, was musty and mouldy. One literally dripped with sweat day and night. The hot dry weather was easier to cope with. There were glorious moonlight nights when it seemed brighter outside than with the uncertain electricity inside. Best of all the too brief 'cold weather' when it was possible to have Christmas lunch in the garden with the sun shining from a cloudless blue sky.

I think travel and weather play such a large part in my memory because in those conditions it took so long to get anything done and so long to get anywhere. They intensified the pressures caused by lack of staff in a developing hospital, and made the not infrequent emergencies all the more desperate. When I returned to Rajshahi in September, 1956, after my first furlough, one emergency followed on another. In early 1957 there was an Asian Flu epidemic which went on for months, during which most of the women nurses were affected and had to have sick leave. That meant being on the go from morning till night, and often into the night. On my birthday I remember Molly Patrick saying to me, "Silver and gold have I none, but I'll give you the weekend off". That really was a present! That year I had a very good holiday in South India - again thanks to Molly standing in. At this time I was living with the Dawsons and I don't think I could have kept going but for Margaret; whatever time I turned up, there was always food and help.

When I met Joyce Saunders off the plane in Calcutta on January 1st, 1958, I thought I could see an end to my frantic life in the hospital. She had to learn the language etc. but it was obvious she was going to fit in. Her arrival meant there were two married couples and four single women on the mission staff, but within a matter of months, for various reasons, only Joyce and I remained. In early 1959 I remember rejoicing because there was a full staff in the hospital, the first time since I returned in 1956. It didn't last long, three weeks later two midwives went down with chicken-pox.

There was also responsibility in the School giving moral support to the Bengali Head Teacher and to those good, friendly and helpful members of staff; it also involved dealing with Government departments, School Inspectresses etc. Both from them and other government officials I met with kindness and helpfulness.

I remember about December, 1958, being in the Operating Theatre from 7.00 a.m. to 10.45 a.m., and then in the School, sitting with the Inspectress through a Diploma Cookery examination from 11a.m. to 5 p.m. There were eleven girls which meant eleven separate wood fires with resulting smoke. Each girl cooked four things and we had to sample them all. Luckily I always had a tough digestive system - but this was a marathon. Then I rushed back to the hospital to give a lecture. The following day there was the School prize-giving with entertainment, accompanied by the usual babel of sound as the mothers etc. talked most of the time - understandable as they rarely had an opportunity to go out and meet other women.

In the hospital, where most of my working hours were spent, as in the WMA bungalow, all water had to be carried in the earlier years, and after use drained into the open drains running round the buildings - except what went into the recently installed septic tanks. In those early days equipment was scarce and all the sheets had either holes in them or had been patched. But even in such primitive conditions many operations were successfully performed, and over the years, with staff, operations and midwifery all increasing, patients came from a wide area. Both Dr Upen Malakar, the first Bengali Superintendent, appointed in 1958, and his wife, Dr Mina Malakar, worked tirelessly for the hospital. They also worried about the health of their missionary colleagues and tried to put a break on our activity.

During those years at Rajshahi there was much else. The joy of seeing the Santal work develop, the beauty of fields of rice, jute, sugar cane, mustard and the lovely flowering trees - all in their seasons a great contrast to the dusty or muddy roads, the squalor and poverty which so often surrounded them. There were the chores of being Mission Council secretary, writing up minutes and related correspondence; and much worse, having to deal with accounts, OM and WMA, which were far from simple. What a relief when they were joined together about 1963! There were the kindnesses and help of colleagues, British and Bengali, on the spot, and those at a distance, WMA branches and people like the Liverpool nurses in the Medical Missionary Association who worked to provide things for the hospital, and those who sent innumerable magazines to keep us in touch with the world outside. And when things got tough, there was Reg Fenn, our OM secretary in London, a tower of strength. I remember one especially bad patch of "emergencies" when it was a letter from him that kept me going.

Joyce Saunders went to East Pakistan in 1958 to work as a nurse in Rajshahi Hospital. She served there till 1965, but then returned home for family reasons. In 1972 she gave a further two years of service at a very difficult time of political change, returning home in 1974.

Contrary to the usual three weeks of sea and land travel, my journey to Rajshahi was by air to Karachi, a change of planes and then on to Calcutta, where I was met by Joan Hope (now Paton). I had been in India as a child so I didn't suffer from culture shock. In fact, when the bearer at the airport rest-house brought in a tray of tea, the apple peel I had left on the cloth was tipped onto the floor for the sweeper to clear away and I thought, "I'm back".

My arrival in Rajshahi was at a turning point in the Hospital's history. The missionary doctor, Ian Patrick, retired and Dr Upen Malakar, the first Bengali Medical Superintendent was appointed. His wife, Dr Mina Malakar, a graduate of Vellore, was also on the staff and quickly gained the respect of the Muslim ladies in the town.

The Hospital consisted of a men's ward, cared for by male nurses; a women's general ward and a maternity ward and two private wards; men's outpatients on one side, and the women's outpatients on the other, behind an "open work" wall so that the women could see out but the men couldn't see in. All the male nurses were trained. On the women's side we had three trained nurses and all the rest were students as we had our own midwifery training school. For years we worked to get it government recognition. Other members of staff were a Path. Lab Technician who did simple stool, urine and blood tests; a Dispenser and his assistant; the Clerk who dealt with outpatients and their notes; the hospital Accountant who dealt with the in-patients' and outpatients' bills; and along with these the male and female sweepers to clean the wards, buckets (each bed had a small bucket to spit into), bedpans (the male nurses refused to touch bedpans), and to wash the babies' nappies etc.

The hospital was different from any I had previously seen. In place of springs on the iron bedsteads there was a metal sheet with ventilation holes, and on top of this, in place of a mattress, was a palliasse. When these became dirty or completely flat and hard, the cover was changed, the straw burnt and fresh straw put in. No one had a top sheet unless they were seriously ill. During the day the patients often sat cross-legged on their beds with the knitted blanket folded down at the bottom of the bed. Most patients poured water over their right hands before eating and rinsed out their mouths; the buckets by each bed were also for the benefit of the "pan" (pronounced parn, betel-leaf) chewers. By the time I arrived there was cold running water, but hot water, when needed, was heated on wood fires outside.

Before operating the surgeon always prayed for help and guidance. Most operations we did were below the chest, and for these the equipment was sterilised in autoclaves heated by four-burner primus stoves (a job I left to the expertise of the male nurses!) Nothing could be done quickly and even for emergency operations it took an hour to prepare the theatre. It was cooled by fans as the electricity was not reliable enough for air-conditioning. When the electricity failed operations had to be completed by torch-light.

The maternity ward was usually full. To encourage the mums to come to the ante-natal clinics they were promised two jackets or woollies for the baby if they attended the clinic twice. This was only possible because we used to receive tea chests full of such useful things for the hospital from England. They stopped when transport charges became too expensive. We also used old Christmas cards - the brighter and shinier the better - from the same source, as a reward to the children for being good when they had to have injections.

Every now and then babies were found abandoned and brought to us to be cared for. We looked after them until a Christian family could be found to adopt them. Others babies, like Komal, were brought, about two years old but only weighing 8lbs 8oz., or another, brought by her mum, six months old but only weighing 6lbs. The mother had no milk and the family cow had died. At that time it wasn't Nestle's baby Formula that was given to babies, it was Robinson's Patent Barley. So this baby was given that. It sparked off a correspondence with Robinson's who finally agreed to put a picture of a cow beside the picture of a tin of Robinson's Patent Barley on the Bengali instruction leaflet.

A notable memory related to the hospital comes to mind. I was cycling home and passed three tall men walking home after a day's work at the hospital. They were chatting happily and looking at the sky, hoping to see the tiniest bit of the moon which would mean the end of Ramadan, the month of fasting. The significant thing was that one man was a Christian, one a Hindu and one a Muslim.

Our church was not a grand looking building - more like a shoe-box with windows, a cross on the roof at one end, and wide steps at the other. The benches had backs to them, and men sat on one side and women and men on the other. Our minister was the Revd P.K.Barui. There was no organ or piano and the School headmistress usually started the singing. One local custom was the bringing of first-fruits from their gardens which were sold on the steps of the church - the proceeds presumably for church funds.

Other memories come to mind. We lived nearly a mile from the hospital and one of the hazards of being called out at night were the goats who liked to sleep on the road and were not always seen by the light of a bicycle lamp. A walk along the road at any time meant being followed by a crowd of men and boys. Then there was the beauty and grandeur of the River Ganges, so near to us, and the contrast between the fine Rajshahi university building and the mud huts. One season we had frequent earth-tremors of which we became aware in different ways. The sparrows in the house went mad and flew round in circles. If you were in bed a tremor sounded as if a trunk was being dragged across the floor, or an underground train going by, or everything rattled. One time, sitting at my desk, the floor felt like mercury and the desk moved, hitting me on one side and then the other. My experience of a cyclone (or tornado) was of a short, sharp shock, but a great clearing up afterwards. By the time I had struggled round the ward closing the shutters, the store-room roof was off, the Land-Rover had been blown out of the car-port, the mahogany tree across the road was blown down and things were blown all over the place.

On my return to Rajshahi in 1972 I recall the remarkable absence of vultures. Seats on coaches could now be booked, no animals were allowed, there were fewer trains, Rajshahi had its own air-strip and the Fokker Friendship had taken the place of the Dakotas. Thanks to our share of relief goods for the hospital, most beds had proper mattresses, and there were enough sheets for the patients to have a top sheet. The mission houses had running (cold) water and there was drinking water from a tube well. There was now a Girls' High School, popular for girls of all religions, on the mission compound. And the last of these memories is that when I left in October,1974, the Children's Ward was nearly completed.

Bob and Pat Irving served in East Pakistan from 1963 to 1966. After their first furlough they were transferred to Malaysia, where Bob served English-speaking congregations in Kota Bharu, Kulai and Johore Bahru. They returned to the UK in 1973 and Bob ministered in Plymouth and Ewell till retirement.

Gone fishing

The Reverend Priya Barui, my Bengali colleague and I decided to go fishing. Like all ministers everywhere, with only one day a week to work, we had plenty of time. Priya told me that he knew where there were magnificent fishing opportunities. A few miles from Rajshahi there was a Hindu Rajah's palace, surrounded by very big man-made lakes which were just teeming with fish. He knew the Rajah's family and he was sure we would be given permission to spend a happy day fishing.

We travelled out by Bengali bus, crowded to the roof tops and with large lumps of inner tube bulging ominously out of one of the front tyres. These were ignored by the driver as he had a more constant worry on his mind. Every few miles he would stop the bus and fill a can from a wayside stream and top up the heavily steaming radiator.

Such minor but by no means unusual incidents did not delay us too much and eventually we arrived at the palace. After partition in 1947 and the creation of the Muslim states of West and East Pakistan most of the Hindu landlords had fled the country. The Rajah, (King) who owned this palace had also gone to Calcutta. His Crown Prince, the Raj-Kumar, remained behind to try to keep some semblance of ownership of their vast possessions.

The palace itself was becoming derelict. Of all its 32 rooms many were nominally occupied by Pakistan Government departments, and the Raj-Kumar and his family stayed in just two. The desolation caused by this tremendous upheaval had left its mark in many ways. The most obvious was the deep scar round the Raj-Kumar's neck where he had once tried to cut his throat.

He greeted Priya and me very graciously and freely gave us permission to fish in the Palace ponds. As is the way of the East we spent quite some time in conversation before going off to fish. He spoke English without the trace of an accent, so in my clumsy Occidental way I asked him where he had gone to school. Priya rushed in to cover up my gauche remark, "Bob, Bob," he said. "These Rajahs were so rich they didn't go to school. They had English tutors come to them and teach them in their palaces". Then, to drive the point of their wealth home, he said, "You know, these Rajahs were so rich they used to eat meat every day."

That stark illustration of the difference in living standards between a wealthy country like ours and Bangladesh occupied my mind throughout the rest of the day and on many days since. So Priya and I went to sit out on the fishing platforms on the lakes. Through the day he interpreted for me the loud and vehement quarrels going on in the village huts around the lake. One man threatened murder on the one in his house or village who had stolen his biro.

Nowadays I have half a dozen ball point pens sent to me by 'Which' magazine, and I eat meat every day.

And at the end of that long day by the palace, Priya and I had not caught a single fish between us, but I had much food for thought.

Witness for Christ

In the English speaking congregation of the Holy Light Church in Johore Bahru, we had many young Asian people, mostly Chinese, who had become Christian. There was however, a frequent problem over baptism. Their parents had no objection to their coming to Church, attending Boys' or Girls' Brigade Bible Class, but they very firmly opposed their being baptised.

In a culture where respect for parents is so highly important, and where the fifth commandment enjoys a similar respect, this caused much heartache.

One day, a young man in the congregation, let's call him Kim, rang me in great distress. His grandfather had died and as the eldest grandson he would be expected not just to attend the funeral but to take part in ceremonies which were seen to be an act of worship of his honourable grandfather.

As a Christian, Kim felt that it would be wrong for him to worship any God but the Lord and Father of our Lord Jesus Christ. He was a timid, shy lad, with a very domineering, aggressive father, who would be furious if Kim disobeyed him. What was he to do?

As a dim-witted foreigner I didn't understand half of what went on in a Chinese funeral, but I did know that the local Christians understood. They said quite clearly that to take part in traditional funeral practices was tantamount to offering not just respect but worship to the spirit of the one who had died.

I knew that, and I knew that Kim would find it very difficult to stand up to his father. I told him it would be best if he simply attended the funeral, to show respect to his grandfather, but that he should not offer worship to the old man's spirit. But if he felt unable to stand up to his father's rage and bullying, and did participate, we would understand, and we would forgive him. And I assured him that God would forgive him too.

After the phone call I rang the church deacons, and I rang the Church prayer circle and told them the situation. Over the next couple of days Kim rang me again several times, and he spoke to many of his Christian friends. We all gave the same message, that if he had to take part in the funeral ceremonies, we would forgive, and we assured him of God's love and forgiveness.

Came the time of the funeral, and Kim went along but told his father that he would not take part in the worshipping ceremonies. His father was outraged and blustered and stormed at the lad but in the end gave way.

A fortnight later that shy, timid lad stood up in front of the congregation and gave his testimony as to the way in which he had been helped to witness for Christ.

Jean Degenhardt served in East Pakistan/Bangladesh from 1970 to 1979, as a nursing sister in the Rajshahi Hospital, but was also a refugee in India during the war between East and West Pakistan. She returned to the UK in 1979 and continued serving through the nursing profession.

My first year as a missionary was a 'Baptism of Fire'! It was full of memorable incidents which included a hurricane, a tidal wave, a war between East and West Pakistan, and being a refugee in India.

I arrived in East Pakistan, as it was then, in October, 1970. It was the end of the monsoon season, very hot, very humid, very wet. I was met in Dhaka by Elizabeth Connan, a missionary doctor of twenty years, and a woman of great character. It was she who had encouraged me to apply for the job of nursing sister in the Rajshahi Hospital where she worked. We flew from Dhaka to Ishurdi, 60 miles from Rajshahi , and then travelled by land-rover on a single track tarmac road to our destination. Rajshahi was a town of 80,000 people, on the banks of the Ganges, which marks the border with India.

Memories of my first views of the land are still very vivid. The land was flat with beautifully lush rice fields interspersed with palm, banana, mango and lichee trees and small villages. The houses, made of mud walls and straw roofs, seemed all so neat and tidy, and purple water hyacinths flourished in the water tanks around which they were gathered. These tanks are used for drinking, washing and sometimes for catching fish. There seemed to be people everywhere, the majority being men and children. Being a Moslem country the women stay indoors and the men go to the market and work in the bazaars and the majority of the businesses. The few village women to be seen were covered in a black cloth called burkas, observing the Moslem custom of not showing either face or figure to other men, and walked behind their husbands. Most of the men wore shirts and lungis, a strip of material which hung like a skirt, and many were barefooted as were the children. Crowds of people will always remind me of Bangladesh, as I soon learnt that everywhere I went people seemed to appear out of nowhere. As foreign, white and a woman one was always a centre of attraction, and at times I found this inhibiting.

My first impression of the mission compound is also a vivid memory; brick houses surrounded by mango and lichee trees and gardens full of flowers. For most of my time in Rajshahi I lived in what had once been a former hospital building and I grew very fond of my sitting room with its lovely balcony overlooking the compound.

I spent the first few months in Barisal, south of Dhaka, at language school learning Bengali, a language with which I constantly struggled over the years. During the first week there we had a tremendous hurricane and were fortunate to be living in a brick building which was able to withstand winds of 120m.p.h.. Later we learnt that there had been a huge tidal wave very close to us which killed thousands of people in the Bay of Bengal. That same night one of the Anglican Fathers in a nearby mission was killed by dacoits - thieves who kill for money. I remember my feelings of shock and also of frustration at my inability to help in any way.

War broke out between East and West Pakistan in March 1971. East Pakistan fought for its independence, and eventually, with India's help became Bangladesh. It was a frightening experience. By then I was back in Rajshahi, and because the situation had become so dangerous it was decided that the majority of women and children, together with Dr Malakar, the medical superintendent of the Hospital should cross over to India and go to Jiaganj, the Mission Hospital in West Bengal; they were to stay there until the shooting and killing stopped. Elaine Morgan and her children, Gareth and Catherine, Elizabth Connan and myself were included in this group, but David Morgan, her husband, remained with some others of the Christian community.

After an eventful trek, which included crossing the Ganges and surviving a tremendous storm, we arrived in Jiaganj. I was able to work among the many refugees who fled to West Bengal and I stayed in a border camp of soldiers who were guarding the border between India and East Pakistan. Memories there are of a cyclone, of living in a little straw hut, and of thousands of people suffering from malnutrition, dysentery, cholera and typhoid .

Because of these traumatic events my expected four year term of service was reduced to one. After furlough I remember finding it difficult to face the prospect of returning in 1972 to a war-torn country which had endured so much suffering, hardship and poverty. However, I also knew that I would be with people of Rajshahi whom I had come to know and love.

During the remaining seven years the work in the Hospital was at times difficult, frustrating, but also rewarding. We received recognition from the Bangladesh Nursing Council to begin a three year general nursing course and a one year midwifery course. Being recognised by the Government in this way gave a great boost to the Hospital. Both a new children's ward and eventually a new nursing school and living quarters were added. My memories of a typical work day are as follows:

7.45 a.m. Started work, having cycled a mile from the mission compound.
8.00 a.m. Joined morning prayers, held in one of the wards.
8.15 a.m. Attended the doctor's rounds of the patients. The majority of the
       patients had tuberculosis, gastric and gynaecological problems.
       Malnutrition and dysentery were also problems.

9 a.m. - 1.00 p.m. Helped to supervise the nurses in their ward work, and assisted in the maternity and female outpatient work.
1.30 - 3.00 p.m. Lunch of curry and short rest in the heat of the day (temp. varied from 30 to 40 degrees centigrade).
3.00 - 7.00 p.m. Helped to supervise the theatre work and often assisted with Caesarean sections, and tubal ligations.
Taught practical nursing to the student nurses.
Assisted in the administration work of the Nursing School.
Took turns to be on call at night for maternity emergencies of which there were many.

Of people there are many who evoke memories, and two I recall with great affection. The first was Asrita's Ma, a Santal tribal lady who cleaned the house for us, petite, and with a lovely, toothless giggle. When I last visited Bangladesh, I met her returning from work on a building site. Her face lit up and she whispered in my ear, 'Have you not found a man yet?' She was always concerned about my single state! The second was Dr.Mrs Khandokar, a Moslem lady doctor who worked in the hospital. She was very committed to the Hospital and was loved and respected by her colleagues and patients alike. Her life was an example to all.

The animal and insect life in all seasons revive less pleasant memories. Mosquitoes, lizards (Tic Tic), snakes, cockroaches, black and red ants, were tolerable, but the war with white ants and with musk rats was an unending struggle. The former devoured everything in their path, except metal, and while the musk rats running round the edge of the rooms and climbing the drain pipes were generally harmless, they did enjoy eating soap and underwear! With them it was a love-hate relationship!

The Church of East Pakistan had barely been formed in 1970 before we became the Church of Bangladesh, and Rajshahi a deanery within it. I have happy memories of prayer meetings, communal picnics, functions arranged by the young people with dancing, singing and sketches. With the Danish Santal Mission a Christian Bookshop was opened in the town, and attracted many enquiries, but it was a struggle to maintain the momentum of witnessing to a sometimes hostile community. The work among the Santals and Hindu community was encouraging, but churches are small and very poor financially, and still need a lot of support.

I have many wonderful and some painful memories. I know that I received much more than I gave, and Bangladesh will always be part of me. It was a privilege to be a serving member of the community there.

David and Elaine Morgan served in East Pakistan (later Bangladesh) from 1961 to 1972, working mainly among the Santal people. After returning to the UK they continued their ministry in Stoke Newington, Milford Haven with Tiers Cross, Hook, Neyland and Rosemarket.

'The best of times and the worst of times' Rajshahi 1961-1972

The years 1961 - 72 were fraught with danger for the people of Rajshahi. Periods of martial law were interspersed with various attempts to build what was called 'guided democracy' which, as it was imposed from above, always failed. Tension between India and Pakistan, never far from breaking point, exploded into brief conflict in 1965. Though the fighting took place in the West, the East too was placed on a war footing, and expatriates were required to leave Rajshahi. When China invaded India her army came perilously close to the Pakistan border before they returned home, as though surprised they had got so far so quickly!

There were communal riots in which those Hindu communities which had not already fled to India were exposed to persecution. The bigoted eye of the fanatic made no distinction between Hindu and Tribal communities and Christians too, whether Tribal or Bengali, lived in fear. Sometimes their fear was justified. Later on tensions between Bengali and Bihari communities were to explode into violence. There were days and nights when the stench of the burnt hair and flesh of humans choked our lungs.

They were also the years in which a rift between West and East Pakistan grew into a yawning, unbridgeable chasm. Student riots would flare into civil war only to be ruthlessly suppressed with great loss of life. The countless graves of Bengali martyrs were laying the foundation of what was to become Bangladesh. Finally, India exploited, for her own advantage, Pakistan's fatal weakness and enabled the East to throw off the West's hated stranglehold. But that only happened after a year of huge disruption in which great numbers of persons became refugees, unknown numbers died, whole villages were razed to the ground and great tracts of the countryside were left uncultivated. Bangladesh was born in blood, tears and almost unimaginable poverty. In the first flush of freedom many said the price had been worth paying.

As though all this were not enough they were also years in which the country was battered by the most appalling natural disasters. A succession of cyclones funnelled their way up the Bay of Bengal, carrying walls of water before them which swept destructively across the fertile delta lands where concentrations of the population lived. Lost lives were counted in hundreds of thousands, some would reckon in millions. Though the full force of these storms had weakened by the time they reached Rajshahi, our District too had to cope with storm damage, flooding and consequent economic chaos and food shortage.

A spectator to these events might be forgiven for thinking that no regular pattern of life could be maintained in such a chaotic kaleidoscope of happenings. But most people, living apart from the urban centres, were only directly affected when disaster struck their particular locality. For them 'normal' life continued come what may. It had to! So did the life of the Church. But even 'normal' life was a struggle against great odds.

These years were 'the best of times and the worst of times' for Elaine, Gareth, Catherine and me. I think they were so too for the people of Rajshahi.

The best of times

We lived on a sprawling mission compound alongside Bengali and Santali families and British compatriots. Neighbours included Danes, Americans and Norwegians. Because Rajshahi had recently become a University town there was, in peaceful times at least, a constant stream of visitors seeking a place to stay. In that remote, isolated town we were immensely privileged! Guests included Kathleen Kenyon, Margaret Miles, and the Bristol Young Vic. Mother Theresa called once but decided to stay somewhere more restful! People would ask us whether we were lonely. But that was the last thing we ever were. In any case the village congregations were less than a day's travel away, and there we always knew that we would be surrounded by friends wanting to talk, to play and to pray.

For Catherine and Gareth it was heaven. They were free to wander and play safely, since they were surrounded by known faces who would not let them come to harm. When night came we would go searching for them and often find them in someone's home put to bed with their Santali or Bengali friends. They grew up speaking Bengali and Santali fluently, though their English was rather less accomplished. Their unvarying custom was to speak Santali to each other, Bengali when required, and English to us. We never heard them confuse their languages.

The Christian community in Rajshahi was representative of many denominations. Christians were drawn to the town to work in the hospital and the high school for which the Church was responsible, or to other work that became available in the growing town. So worshippers at the Sunday service far outnumbered actual members of the church, and the more forceful leaders in the community were not always able to participate formally in decisions. When India and Pakistan briefly went to war in 1965, and foreign nationals were excluded from the border area, the community met the emergency by agreeing that all its worshipping members would be full members of the Rajshahi United Church, without being required to give up their membership of their 'home' churches. It was a practical and fruitful decision that smoothed the path to wider union when in 1971 the Rajshahi United Church entered the Church of Pakistan, which in a matter of months, through political necessity, became the Church of Bangladesh.

As the years passed, my participation in the management of the Hospital and the High School increased, but my first responsibility was to the scattered Santal communities of Christians in Rajshahi, Kharmarmaria, Shibpur, Nosrotpur, Pailorpukor, Belghoria and Jalalabad. When in the crisis of 1971, practically the whole of the Rajshahi congregation became refugees in India, it was the strong ties of friendship and ministry with these wonderful people that made it impossible for me to leave.

Our hope for the Santal congregations was threefold: [1] to nurture their Christian faith as the generation that had made its 'decision for Christ' was succeeded by a second generation that was growing up in the church; [2] to enable the children to receive a basic education in their own language so that those who moved on to study in Bengali at a later stage would not be too disadvantaged; and [3] to give these most poor and hard working people security by enabling them through loan funds to own land for themselves. It was an uphill struggle! Against a background of economic hardship, political uncertainty, war and natural disaster, families were torn between a desire to flee for their lives and stay to protect the little they had.

But some of the best times of my life were spent in their company. When we went as a family as we frequently did, eating as they ate and sleeping as they slept, barriers of race and money and education seemed to crumble to nothing as the hours passed in story telling, teasing, laughing and prayer. Sometimes I have been asked what my chief memory of those years is. Some of the sad ones follow, but chief of all is a feeling of joy and harmony on entering a Santal village after walking or cycling many miles to get there, and being greeted with frank and open smiles of welcome, the laughter of children playing and the sounds of village life.

The worst of times

Jalalabad was the largest of the congregations. The village always seemed to be bursting with children! In a time of communal riots and movement of population, with the promise of land settlement in India dangled before them, the community moved across the border lock, stock and barrel, leaving only the growing crops in the fields for others to harvest. I walked through the empty ghost village in despair, my hopes of a flourishing settled Christian community dashed by their dispersal. I returned eighteen months later and it was as though no one had ever lived there, their mud houses now ploughed into the ground for cultivation. Only the fruit trees remained as evidence of the life there once had been.

Rajshahi was a ghost town. A battle had been fought over it. Mortars had exploded around the house, mercifully missing it. The bulk of the town population, including most Christians had become refugees in India. The Pakistan army had reoccupied the town, in the process shooting everyone they encountered. Bodies were left to lie where they fell at the road side - it would be almost a year before the bleached bones would be buried. I had become separated from the family; it was to be some time before I learnt that Elaine, with great courage, had taken the children on a horrendous, frightening journey across the Ganges to safety in India. I had never felt more frightened and homesick. As dawn broke that morning, just as every other morning, the call went up from the mosque: "God is great. God is great. I bear witness that there is no God but God. Come to prayer!" I had thought the town to be empty of people and God forsaken. It took a faithful Muslim to teach me otherwise.

Years after we had settled back in Britain I was leading worship on Good Friday when, unaccountably (as it seemed then) and for the first time in my life, I broke down in tears as I read the story of the Crucifixion of our Lord. As I later reflected on what had happened I realised that at a level other than conscious thought I had made in that moment an emotional connection between Jesus' Passion and the sufferings of the people of Bengal during the time we lived among them. Tears, pent at the time, flowed out of control. One memory, in particular, haunts me. In the hysteria of the weeks following the defeat of the Pakistan army when ordinary people were wreaking their vengeance on 'collaborators' (real or imagined) I met in the road a mob that was dragging along one such 'traitor'. His arms, bound to a heavy length of bamboo, were held out horizontally so that his figure made the shape of a cross. Passers-by hurled pieces of brick at him, or spat at him; some ran up and kicked him so that he stumbled and fell; his face, ashen grey, showed no feeling. He was moments from death. As I watched, as people had watched Jesus carry his cross all those years ago, I understood that Jesus' suffering face must have been identical to his. There is then no way of distinguishing any suffering human face from the face of our Lord.

I place on record my thanks to Christians in Rajshahi, Bengali and Santali, who took us to themselves in a kind of love/hate relationship for all that we represented of our imperial and racialist history and all that we were as Christian brothers and sisters, strangers and guests; who when we were frightened helped us find courage; and when we were hungry helped us find food; who led us, at least part way, out of a narrow, western, tunnel vision of God's world.

I cannot tell how significant those years were for the future of the Church in Bangladesh. The passage of time alone will be able to demonstrate that. One thing I learnt was that a few committed people can accomplish remarkable things. The Church should never be afraid of being small.

Belghoria Church and Preacher's House

Pilgrims in Mission   *Thanksgiving Service*

Celebrating 150 years of the English Presbyterian Mission
Wednesday 9 July, 1997
United Reformed Church General Assembly, Portsmouth

Introduction

Opening Hymn 573   God is working his purpose out

South Fujian, Xiamen (Amoy) – Where the Mission Began
Revd Ian R M Latto (South Fujian, 1935-51)
    In 1850 the English Presbyterian Mission decided on Amoy as a centre to begin work in China, following some evangelistic visits by William Burns and Dr. Young. From there by the grace of God the work spread.
    In 1935 conditions in South Fujian seemed to be settling after periods of unrest. Our Mission was seriously understaffed as three of us went out – Reg Mobbs to the southern district around Changpu, Miss Kathleen Duncan to teach in Chuanchow, and myself to Yungchun. The EPM (English Presbyterian Mission) here had recently taken oversight from formerly Methodist Episcopal Mission of three rural, mountainous counties. This added the latest Presbytery of Eng-Tek-Tai to South Fujian Synod. Mrs Jett transferred to our WMA (Women's Missionary Association) and stayed on in Yungchun.
    In May 1938 the Japanese bombed and occupied the island of Amoy and Mrs Jett, on her way back from furlough, was held up several weeks in the international settlement of Kulangsu and aided our Amoy staff who did splendid relief work among the refugees who had sought safety there.
    As the Japanese made no further advance, work continued almost as usual though all motor roads were broken up and travel had to be on foot, boat or bicycle. Churches were growing in membership and in Yungchun were further aided spiritually by weeks of revival meetings. In all areas the schools showed most rapid growth.
    There were occasional bombing raids:- South Street Church in Chuanchow, our primary school in Tehwa, Talmage Theological College, temporarily used as a hospital – but worst, the Changpu hospital and compound, in which Reg Mobbs narrowly escaped with his life. Some of our

schools then evacuated, - Chuanchow Pei-Yuan school (Westminster College) evacuated to Kau-to, and Yungchun Chong-Hian Middle School moved further up in the hills. Our hospital in Chuanchow was very short staffed, doctors being sought from other sources, until in 1940, Drs. Landsborough and Tunnell and Miss Keningale arrived.

After the Pearl Harbour disaster in 1941 our Amoy staff were house-interned by the Japanese until exchanged for Japanese nationals in Allied hands.

In 1942 the South Fukian Synod met and celebrated the centenary of the arrival of the first missionary in this Province, the American Revd Abeel. (Eight years before Wm. Burns and Dr. Young arrived in 1850.) At this Synod the principles of the 3-self Church were accepted, though Eng-Tek-Tai Presbytery was exempted from self-support as it was the poorest financially. Work began on the document to hand over mission property and define the position of the missionary.

In 1944 some of us managed, before the Japanese surrounded our province, to leave China by way of Kunming to take long overdue furloughs. The Doctors remained in Chuanchow with Mr Rogers until the war ended.

On my return in 1946 a drought plus galloping inflation caused the cost of living to fall burdensomely on the churches and pastors. Mrs Jett was now on her own in Yungchun; I remained in Chuanchow assisting with our work in churches and schools; also as we had no staff in the south area, I visited Changpu, Unsio and Chiau-An near the Kwangtung border. District Youth Conferences were enthusiastic and gained splendid attendances.

At the end of August 1949 the communist soldiers peacefully entered Chuanchow. Foreigners then needed police permission to leave the city so work was curtailed. As eventually we had to leave we left knowing that the church, though apprehensive, was in good spirit and the young people confident to maintain their Christian faith and discipleship. Praise God for the excellent witness of that Church today!

East Guangdong, Shantou (Swatow) – Hakka, the next step
Revd George A Hood (Shantou, 1945-50 and Singapore-Malaysia, 1951-72)

William Burns had spent some months in Swatow in 1856 but George Smith who moved there from Amoy in 1858 is rightly regarded as the pioneer of the English Presbyterian Mission in that area.

I suppose my own missionary experience began in earnest when I married into one of those families which have been such a feature of the

English Presbyterian Mission in each of its fields. In my case it was the Duffus-James family which has had a three generation connection with the Swatow-Hakka field in East Guangdong.

But the timing was also significant. I went out to China in the spring of 1945, just when the war in the west ended but we were still expecting to have two more years of war with Japan. I was in Kunming, south-west China, working in the evacuated universities YMCA centre when the war came to its sudden end. I can remember being a standing passenger on a bus on my way to teach an English class in a factory outside Kunming when the news of that strange bomb with its devastating effects was on everyone's lips.

The end of the war enabled Beth to catch up with me and we arrived in Swatow together in time for Christmas 1945 to serve out our full five year term.

It was a time of relief work, rehabilitation and re-opening of institutions, schools, hospitals, theological college and churches, all of which had suffered badly in the war and Japanese occupation of a large area of the field. We were full of hope, and the civil war, resumed in 1947, at first seemed a long way off. As it came nearer, and the local guerrillas more active, there was still hope, mingled with apprehension, of a new China in place of the discredited and corrupt regime which had already betrayed so many hopes. The last few months in the summer of 1949, before the take-over, were somewhat fraught. And that strange, almost silent twenty four hours between the departure of the old and the arrival of the new rulers will always be remembered.

For the next year we learned to live under a new regime in an atmosphere where the idealism of the young was tempered by the caution of the old. The Church's institutions continued to function and we completed in mid 1950 our first full term of service. When the time came to leave I had hopes of returning to China and the Swatow police assured me – "no problem". But that very week the Korean War began, positions became quickly polarised, and what might have been a gradual withdrawal of missionary presence became a rapid one.

As you know, for thirty years we had no contact with these earliest fields of our missionary endeavour. When China opened its doors again – and this time by her own choice – we had the joy of renewed contact and fellowship. It has been the greatest of joys and a privilege – a real bonus in retirement – to visit China as a friend and to be assured that the friendships formed in those early years of our missionary experience have continued –

to be able to share the joy and happiness and above all the hopes of our Chinese brothers and sisters in Christ. Our joy is tinged with sadness that so many of our older colleagues, who had given a whole life-time in service, did not live to see, as we have done, the Church as it is today – a Church not without problems, but one that is full of faith, hope and love.

Revd Su De-ci, General Secretary, China Christian Council
The Church in China Today

At this special thanksgiving service marking the 150th anniversary of the EPM I would like to share with you the situation of the Protestant Church in mainland China today in order to give witness to the presence of God among us and express thanks for those EPM missionaries who had sown seeds of life in China.

In the beginning years of the 1950s our church in mainland China was facing a crisis of survival, but God did not forsake us. It was due to the revelation God gives us that the Three-self Movement came into being. The movement gave us a political position on the side of the Chinese people. It also tested our spirituality and turned the Church in China into a Self with commitment to God.

It is well known that the Protestant Church in China had undergone during the Cultural Revolution a valley of the shadow of death, but in the seventeen years since the reopening of the Church in mainland China She has become not only a recovered Church, but also a renovated Self.

We see a great leap in the number of Christians in China from 700,000 in 1949 to more than ten million now. Forty thousand churches and meeting points have been built, rebuilt or recovered. More than eighteen million copies of the Bible have been published. Twelve theological colleges and five Bible schools were established, as well as a great number of training centres. We are poor and weak, but the almighty God showed God's power over our weakness and God's richness over our poverty. Seeing all this we should offer thanksgiving out of sincerity, and resolve to continue to give mighty witness to God's name.

Though evangelism had been made use of by colonialism and left some traces of dishonour on Chinese soil, we are still grateful to most of the missionaries for bringing the gospel to China. We will never forget their achievements, "How beautiful upon the mountains are the feet of those who proclaim the good news." The Holy Spirit works to train Christians in China. They have now carried on the responsibility of proclaiming the gospel and constructing the Church in China. They are authors of a new

page of history of the Protestant Church in China. Due to her adherence to the Three-Self principle she has shown her particularity in the family of the Church Ecumenical which also enriches the catholicity of the big family.
We are limbs of the same body of Christ. Let us build and bless each other through mutual care and prayers. We extend best wishes for the Church both in Britain and China and wish the missionaries here present the bliss of long life.

Litany
Lighting of a candle
Sung response: "Kindle a flame…"
Leader: Let us thank God for those who served the Gospel in
    South Fujian and East Guangdong
    Congregation: working your purpose out
Leader: for the far and wide preaching ministry of William Burns
    the leadership of Carstairs Douglas in Amoy
    the pioneering spirit of George Smith in Swatow
Congregation: carrying your purpose forward
Leader: for the early missionaries to the Hakka people
    for Catherine Ricketts, first of nearly two hundred
    WMA missionaries
Congregation: making your purpose a reality
Leader: for all who have followed: pastors, teachers, healers,
    facing times of discouragement and danger;
    cherishing the vision of a single Chinese Church;
    maintaining trust and friendship throughout the silent years;
    and for all deeds of courage and commitment
Congregation: fulfilling your purpose in love
Leader: for advocates, administrators, benefactors
    in the churches here
Congregation: enabling your purpose to be resourced
Leader: We thank you for the joy of contacts renewed;
    for past and present growth in membership and mission
    for leadership training of ministry and laity;
    for the work of the China Christian Council
    and the Amity Foundation

Congregation: discovering your purposes afresh
Leader: kindle praise in our hearts,
energy in our lives
and a passion for your Gospel
Congregation: working your purpose out today.

Taiwan – Into its second century
Revd Elizabeth J Brown (Taiwan 1961-89)
In 1965 the Presbyterian Church of Formosa celebrated its centenary. It was a time of great rejoicing – the climax of the Double the Church Movement to double the number of congregations and church members as a thanksgiving offering to God. Guests came from overseas, especially from the so-called 'Mother Churches' in England and Canada. At that time, out of a total of 70 missionaries working with the Presbyterian Church of Formosa, fifteen were English Presbyterians.

By 1985 both the national and the missionary situation had changed. The church name had become the Presbyterian Church in Taiwan. Industrialisation, urbanisation – the 'economic miracle' had taken hold. Travel overseas had become possible. The church had, after long consideration and prayerful seeking of God's will, taken sacrificial steps which had cracked the hard shell of the one-party state. Shoots of democracy were pushing through and burgeoning into life. At that time out of 41 missionaries from thirteen missionary groups working directly under the Presbyterian Church in Taiwan four were from CWM. And the work of the Church had broadened out immensely in evangelism and social concern for minorities.

In the intervening twenty years significant shifts of power and responsibility had taken place from England to Taiwan. Firstly, instead of funds being designated in London for specific projects in Taiwan the Presbyterian Church in Taiwan received a block grant to divide up and use according to its own needs and priorities. Secondly, information about, and communications concerning, the church in Taiwan ceased to be routed via the missionaries but was sent directly from the *office of the Presbyterian Church in Taiwan. The General Assembly Missionary Personnel Committee, which was mostly Taiwanese in membership, had taken over responsibility for looking after missionaries – establishing work priorities, arranging language training and orientation and for providing pastoral care for what was a diverse group of missionaries from a variety of cultural backgrounds.*

All this happened in the midst of dealing with tremendous social change and government harassment which were, in themselves, more than enough to be getting on with.

I first went to Formosa in 1961 as a young woman called to share my gifts with the church and people there. I returned from Taiwan in 1989 older certainly, wiser maybe, realising that my life had been tremendously enriched and that I had received far more than I was ever able to give.

A Church's view of the English Presbyterian Mission
Revd C. S.Yang, General Secretary, Presbyterian Church in Taiwan

"But greater than all other contributions has been Scotland's gift of missionaries to the East – men with a glorious religious heritage, based on the faith of the Covenanters and the Calvinistic creed: men who...propagated the Gospel and built up churches in distant lands: men of faith who faced unknown dangers: men of vocation who stuck to their task and refused to let go until God had blessed them and the people whom they came to serve".

So writes Edward Band in the opening chapter of his book Barclay of Formosa (1936). Today the United Reformed Church gathers to celebrate and thank God for such men and women of conviction, who 150 years ago, began to leave the shores of Great Britain to venture into the unknown. Some for a few years, others like Thomas Barclay, for a lifetime but each with a common purpose to share the good news of God's love and to serve His children.

Historically wherever the early missionaries took the good news they also introduced education and medicine, in this respect the PCE was no exception. Because of the Christian missionaries the Taiwanese were first exposed to modern knowledge, science, medicine, democracy, socialism, western culture etc., beginning with Dr James L. Maxwell 132 years ago. PCT takes pride in being the pioneer of many firsts – the first hospital, first school and first printing press in Taiwan were all established by the Presbyterian Church. The pioneer spirit is still evident as PCT responds to current needs of our fast changing society by caring for political prisoners, women/children slaves of prostitution, exploited fishermen, senior citizens and hospice care.

While such contributions are extremely important to the so-called modern development of our church and our nation, nothing can surpass the personal dedication and sacrifice of individual foreign missionary

Pilgrims in Mission   *Thanksgiving Service*

personnel. The impact of their Christian attributes on our people and our dignity, they liberated our women from bound feet, they opened our minds, they healed our bodies, they challenged our hearts, they stood alongside us in our sufferings, identified with our pains and praised God with us in our triumphs.

Today we gather to give thanks, to rejoice and to celebrate the lives of all the missionary men and women of faith and 'vocation who stuck to their task and refused to let go...' It is to their credit that the Presbyterian Church in Taiwan has long become of age. As we approach the year 2000 the PCT stands firm, an autonomous church, whose mission continues to embrace both evangelism and social concern, and is active in the ecumenical and global family.

We Give Thanks to God for Our Common History of Yesterday
We Rejoice and Affirm Our Common Faith in the Living God Today
We Celebrate Our Common Heritage in Christ Jesus for Tomorrow

Now to him who is able to do immeasurably more than all we ask or imagine, according to his power that is at work within us, to him be Glory in the church and in Christ Jesus throughout all generations, forever and ever. Amen. (Ephesians 3:20-21)

Litany
The lighting of a candle
Sung response: "Kindle a flame..."

Leader: Let us thank God for those who served the Gospel in Taiwan
Congregation: O Lord, you are the life of the world
Leader: for pioneering outreach by the Amoy missionaries
Congregation: O Lord, you make us lamps of new light
Leader: for medical work initiated by James Maxwell
        coming alongside people of all backgrounds
        and providing a ministry of healing love to the
        present day
Congregation: so in the darkest and suffering places lamps shine for you
Leader: We praise you for Thomas Barclay, serving over sixty years;
        for his vision in founding and developing
        Tainan Theological College,

through which ministers, teachers and musicians
have enriched the Church
Congregation: springs of new life for a thirsty people
Leader: We recall warmly how children's imagination
was kindled and people in our own island
were joined in understanding, encouragement and
support
Congregation: springs of new life for a crying people
Leader: We rejoice in the gathering into Christian fellowship
of the mountain peoples
for courageous concern for human rights
and the determination of the church to serve all
peoples
Congregation: lamps in dark place
Leader: As we rejoice to see zeal for evangelism,
joy in proclamation
music and song on the lips of your people,
and the horizons of mission expanded in hope
**Congregation: come live within us
come and enrich us
until we live like you**

Hymn 582   Thanks be to God, whose Church on earth

Singapore and Malaysia – Churches taking root
Revd John S Henderson (Singapore-Malaysia, 1950-77)
When did the seed of the Church put down roots? British and Chinese missionaries had been at work in Singapore and Malaya for many years. But I think that it was in the dark days of the Japanese occupation that it put down roots. During that time the lay leaders of the Churches, and the missionaries who were in internment camps dared to dream! The missionaries planned to open a united theological college after the war. That dream was fulfilled – just as well, as the supply of ministers and preachers from China was cut off when the Communists seized power. The Church had to produce its own ministers. The lay leaders also planned. They knew that the non-Christians with their large ornate temples looked down on the smaller plain Christian worship halls.
When the only two Presbyterian missionaries who survived came out of

internment they discovered that the Church had survived too. The Church leaders soon began to carry out their plans of building new and bigger churches. Now they could do what the temples did on the birthdays of their gods, providing free lavish public entertainment. At Christmas the Churches invited anyone who wanted to come to hear, and see in drama, the story of the birth of <u>their</u> God. And what about fruits from the shoots which sprang up after the war? The Communist insurrection in the Malayan jungle provided a grand opportunity to spread the good news of Jesus Christ to many who had never heard it. The Government in Malaya moved the scattered rural population into so-called 'New Villages' for their safety. The Protestant Churches got together and put a Christian presence into nearly all of these New Villages. Some of the young people who became Christians there later became students at the new theological colleges.

My colleague, George Hood, carried out a survey of the new Christians in our Churches throughout Malaya. He found that over half of the new members had come to faith in Christ, not through evangelistic campaigns, but through friendship of their Christian neighbours or work colleagues. Was not that spirit of friendship perhaps the most fragrant fruit to come from the rooting in times of adversity? Later there were fruits from the overseas work started by both Singaporean and Malaysian Churches. It has been done not only by the Chinese language Churches but also by the English language ones. Time fails for me to tell of the rapid spread of the Gospel among English speaking Asians in both Singapore and Malaysia. But you will have the evidence of the strong growing English language Churches before your very eyes – in the person of the Revd Wong Fong Yang whom you will hear speak soon. He is the first minister of an English language Church to be elected Moderator for the whole Presbyterian Church in Malaysia..

Facing the challenge in Singapore
Revd Richard Teo Ee Hock, Vice-Moderator, Presbyterian Church in Singapore
While we thank God for the legacy of the Presbyterian missionaries we need to pray for present day Singapore. In the process of keeping up with modernisation, society is paying a price, and church life is also profoundly affected. In many ways the pervasive culture of modernisation legitimises the pursuit of materialistic achievements. This current of secularisation is driving the younger generation of Christians to abandon their mission. Riding on the strong social current of modernity it will be a great task to

maintain faithfulness to God's ordinances. The challenges we face are as follows:

To take the emphasis off pursuing higher qualifications at all costs and allow time for prayer meetings and Bible studies requires strong conviction and determination.

Maintaining spirituality is a great challenge in our pluralized society. We have to balance being non-offensive with being the "light of the world" and in every endeavour we should preach the Gospel of racial and religious harmony.

Versatility as a result of mastery over modern technologies enables the younger generation to switch easily from job to job, but this culture of personal confidence emboldens them to challenge the ancient norms of remaining faithful to one's company, one's friends and even spouses. Commitment and dedication are traits we are losing and indifference and non-caring are emerging traits in today's youth. The church faces a great challenge to build not only a "user friendly church" but also an environment where care and compassion are taught.

Facing the challenge in Malaysia
Revd Wong Fong Yang, Moderator, Presbyterian Church in Malaysia

The missionaries from the Presbyterian Church of England had all left Malaysia in the early seventies and the entire leadership of the Presbyterian Church in Malaysia since then comes from its own country. Today we have approximately 90 churches (including preaching stations), 22 ministers, 50 preachers and a communicant membership of 7000. Although the growth of the Presbyterian Church is not spectacular in comparison with Methodist, Basel and Anglican denominations, nevertheless it remains steadfast.

The vision of the Presbyterian Church in Malaysia is to establish 100 churches and achieve 10,000 members by the year 2000AD. The target is not beyond reach. The recent Synod Exco meeting has allocated a substantial amount of money to each Presbytery for church planting work, and each Presbytery has bold plans for such work. The missionaries from the West planted the indigenous church. Their footprints may be seen crisscrossing our country. The Malaysian Presbyterian Church leaders merely continue along the path which the missionaries had opened.

There is a great enthusiasm to plant churches at strategic localities in towns and cities. For many years church planting was centred in rural areas. Rural migration to urban areas poses a serious problem to the rural churches. Many of our youth are working in cities. Hence the need to plant the church in the cities. Church planting is a great challenge in Malaysia and it receives the first priority. However, the greater challenge remains somewhere else.

The year 1990 marked a watershed for the English speaking Presbytery of the Presbyterian Church in Malaysia. It was the year one of its English speaking churches ventured into cross-cultural mission among the Ibans in the interior of Sarawak. Since then four English speaking churches have planted several Iban churches. The spin-off from the partnership with the Sidang Injil Borneo (SIB) denomination is that the English speaking Presbyterian churches have also started six Malay speaking services in Peninsular Malaysia. The SIB seconded some of their workers to help in the work. The Malay language ministry is reaching out not only to the Ibans but also to the Indonesian immigrants and workers in the towns and villages.

The '90s is the decade of mission for the English speaking Presbytery. Anbalangan, from Kluang Agape Presbyterian Church was commissioned as its first missionary in Cambodia in 1992. Dr Choo Yew On and Dr Ling Chern Chern from the Trengganu Presbyterian Church joined OMF to serve as missionary dentists in Cambodia. They were commissioned in 1995. In the same year Beacon Presbyterian church, a relatively young church also sent its first missionaries Chee Hoe and Alice to work in South Asia. Sea Park Presbyterian church could boast of three missionaries, namely Koh Soo Choon, Koh Kok Eng an Lim Geok Seng who work in Afghanistan, Pakistan and China respectively. It is strange that for more than 100 years of its existence the Presbyterian Church in Malaysia has not started its foreign mission - it is a recent phenomenon. As a denomination, the Presbyterian Church in Malaysia has the financial resources and the organisational capability to set up its own mission agency. In a sense we have kept the gospel to ourselves. We have a debt to pay.

The doors of opportunity for mission are wide open. The torch of the gospel which the missionaries brought to us must be passed on. Church planting within Malaysia is a great challenge but the greater challenge is to plant indigenous churches beyond Malaysia. Setting up the Presbyterian Church in Malaysia Foreign Mission agency is the first step towards fulfilling a larger vision.

Litany
Lighting of a candle
Sung response: "Kindle a flame..."

Leader: Let us thank God
for those who served the Gospel in Singapore and Malaysia

Congregation: stepping out in faith
Leader: for the first appointed missionary, John Bethune Cook,
who served for forty years mainly on his own,
drawing on the experience of others.
but single-minded to achieve a self-supporting Church.

Congregation: holding on to faith
Leader: for all who suffered through Japanese internment,
and those who died in prison camps:
Margaret Dryburgh from Singapore,
Ann Livingston and Sabine Mackintosh from Taiwan

Congregation: shining examples of faith
Leader: We marvel at the resilience of these churches,
of Christian families victimised under Japanese occupation,
of communities broken but recreated during armed struggle,
seizing opportunities for extension and growth.

Congregation: victorious faith tested in the fire
Leader: We commend to God the Presbyterian Church in Singapore
its leaders and congregations and schools,
planning for further growth,
serving new needs in a rapidly changing society

Congregation: rediscovering faith for today
Leader: We commend to God the Gereja Presbyterian Malaysia
its widely scattered congregations, urban and rural,
its multi-lingual services and mission outreach
now in a more stable and prosperous environment,
training young people in discipleship and leadership.

Pilgrims in Mission *Thanksgiving Service*

Congregation: faith alive and active
gift of an eternal source
renewed for every generation.
To God be glory for ever.

Rajshahi, Bangladesh – A Christian presence
Mrs Margaret Macleod (Rajshahi/Naogaon, 1938-55)
The first missionary of the Presbyterian Church of England to work in India went to the town and district of Rajshahi in Bengal in 1862. Starting from those early days the Christian work of evangelism, teaching, preaching, the education of children in schools and fine medical work in hospital and district has been carried on and has grown.

The population was Hindu and Muslim, but after the partition of India in 1947 thousands of Hindus left East Pakistan and crossed the border into India. That was an evil time of killing and destruction. Afterwards much rethinking and retraining was done to prepare Christian workers for the increased challenge of Islam.

More recently, in the 1950s, work was started among tribal people, Santals, who received the gospel gladly. In the space of two years or so a small group was asking for baptism. From this beginning 'the Good News' spread to other Santal villages in the area who then asked for teaching. This work, though hard and requiring constant travelling, has given the workers the most encouragement for many years. And the Church grows.

I have been asked to say something about the Women's Missionary Association of which I was President in the 1960s. The contribution of women missionaries (chosen by women and supported by women) was a vital part of the Church. The WMA was started by women of the Presbyterian Church of England in 1878. They felt that full-time women workers were needed to reach women and girls.

The WMA merged with the Overseas Mission Committee in the 1960s and now the work is cared for by the Council for World Mission. Let us remember with gratitude the workers of the WMA, 150 or more, who served in China, Taiwan, Singapore and Malaysia, India and Pakistan.

In the missionary enterprise of the last 150 years missionary wives also had a role to play – and some a more important role than others. In the records and reports of the overseas work you may have noticed in the lists of missionaries, a number of asterisks against some names. This indicated that the man had a wife! I was an asterisk – I was a star! My time, eighteen years, in rural India, then Pakistan was spent mostly in the area of Naogaon, sixty five miles and a long train journey from Rajshahi.

First of all I had to learn the language or stay silent and I had to learn about Islam. Much of my task was running our home, taking on the children's schooling until ten years old when they returned to England.

Tropical illnesses, malaria and others, were common and a doctor was many hours away. (The splendid medical work done in the Naogaon area by the doctors Morison and Macdonald Smith at the beginning of the century was discontinued in the 1920s for lack of support.)

As for our home – the simple life was never simple! We had no running water or other amenities of modern life. During the war years of 1939-45 our isolated home was used for leave and 'comic relief' by many in the armed forces of Britain and the USA. In the famine of 1943 (and after) when two and a half million people died our local Christian community played a valuable part in caring for the sick, the destitute and many orphans. Our home became the distribution centre for rationed essentials, particularly rice which made mountains on our verandah.

In the work of home and church we were part of that small Christian community trying to maintain a Christian presence in the Muslim population around us. Through the years, in times of encouragement and times of failure, we always felt we were where God wanted us to be. We thanked God for that and we honoured the English Presbyterian Mission for their support.

Fellowship in the Gospel
Rt Revd B D Mondal, Bishop of Dhaka, Church of Bangladesh

On this auspicious occasion of the 150th anniversary of the English Presbyterian Mission, we from the Church of Bangladesh extend our heartfelt greetings to all present here and salute those living and deceased who had laboured in the vineyard of God in the north west part of Bangladesh called Rajshahi and all those who were associated in England and in the various Mission fields to give us the opportunity to celebrate the 150th anniversary year today.

According to available records the work of the English Presbyterian Mission in the Rajshahi area was started in 1862 by Revd Beharilal Singh, someone from the sub-continent, a Rajput. He started some schools to establish a relationship with the communities around and was an enthusiastic preacher, organiser and builder. Due to his tireless enthusiasm however he lost his health and died at an early age.

Dr. Donald Morison followed him in 1877. He shifted everything to medical work and worked unrelentingly for 22 year and because of overwork and perhaps from the heat and humid weather also he died of broken health.

In 1900 came Revd Hamilton, Dr. Mcdonald Smith and Miss Miller and a little later Dr. Donald Morison's son, Dr. Robert Morison to join the team. And the procession of dedicated service of many went on until today the McLeods, Dawsons, Georges, Patricks, Connan, Morgans and many others present here from the UK, and people like Priokummar Baroi, Dr. Upen Malakar, Chunka Tudu and others. Now, however, the EPM does not exist. We have a mission doctor couple from a sister church, the Presbyterian Church USA, and we also have someone from the Reformed Churches in the Netherlands, Maria Gosker.

What were the main features of this mission? Their programmes were geared to the spreading of the kingdom of God at any cost and they would change locations and tactics tirelessly as and when the situation dictated. They had great enthusiasm to spread Christianity among Bengali people, especially among Muslims and so we still have names like Mujib, Noor and Rahim, who were converts from Islam and some others. And the Islam of this area was and is in no way tolerant to mission work. It is rather conservative and militant and many of the Islamic Saints, Darvish and Shahs were actual fighters in arms. So there were many risks and setbacks. At a later stage the work among Santali aboriginal people began and flourished because of the loving care they took of them.

Most missionaries were highly educated and able people but were not sparing in their lives, they were enthusiastic about the mission of God. From burial records in those days it has been found that the average life expectancy for expatriates was 26 years. It was surely a daunting reality to be a participant of this kind of history

Those who came were concerned about the welfare of those who joined the church. They tried to make sure that they would settle in to some work or improve themselves. Often they went out of their way acting almost like fathers and mothers to the converts like many other missionary societies and indeed St Paul in 1 Thessalonians 2:6-12. In Bangladesh the EPM was a pioneer for church union like in the case of the CSI and CNI.

In the providence of God this has been a love marriage between the East and the West in one corner of the world. The disbanding of a mission does not and cannot wipe out the memories of these great sons and daughters of God, who like in the Book of Hebrews shine in great splendour *in the hearts of the people of Bangladesh and elsewhere. We who work in those vineyards receive succour and strength through their memories and the love they showered on many living amidst the dark realities of life. They pinpoint something beyond stark facts of our everyday hustle and bustle. May God grant those who left his world rest and fulfilment in his kingdom and also strength for us to run the race that is set before us in their footsteps.*

Litany
Lighting of a candle
Sung response: "Kindle a flame…"

Leader: Let us thank God
for those who served the Gospel in Rajshahi and Naogaon
**Congregation: from utmost east to utmost west
where human feet have trod**
Leader: for the Revd Behari Lal Singh and Mrs Singh
who pioneered mission work in the Rajshahi region,
opening schools and an orphanage,
proclaiming the Good News with courage and energy.
**Congregation: by the voice of many messengers
goes forth the voice of God**
Leader: Let us thank God for all who followed them;
doctors and nurses, teachers and pastors
**Congregation: that light of the glorious Gospel of truth
might shine throughout the world**
Leader: Let us thank God that this Christian presence
struggled and survived over so many years
offering service, worship and witness
in spite of famine and disease,
through times of religious, political and ethnic tension.
**Congregation: vainly we hope for the harvest tide
till God awakens the seed.**
Leader: We pray for the Church of Bangladesh today
developing its life and outreach,
an ark of hope in times of flood,

a creator of new beginnings after disaster has struck,
ecumenically active within its borders and beyond.
**Congregation: that the earth may be filled with the glory of God
as the waters cover the sea.**

PRAYER OF COMMITMENT

God,
the same, yesterday, today and for ever,
we recall past vision and struggle,
past courage and commitment,
in gratitude and wonder.
Take these same bodies and minds,
these hands and hearts,
which we each possess as gifts from you
and fill them with your Spirit
so that wherever we live and travel
your voice is heard
your forgiveness is offered
and your world is transformed
to the eternal glory of your name,
through Jesus Christ our Lord.
Amen!

Closing Hymn 579   Lord, thy Church on earth is seeking

Blessing

List of Missionaries

In most cases the first names of wives have been added. Names in brackets are those following marriage. As far as possible the dates given are those of service on the field - periods of temporary absence or of internment are included. Those whose service began before and continued to 1947 and beyond are recorded along with all who began in or after 1947.

South Fujian

Mr R Tully, Kathlyn	1922-51	Amoy	Educational
Mr & Mrs P Anderson	1933-47	Amoy	Educational
Revd I R M Latto, Joyce	1935-50	Yungchun	Pastoral
Dr D Landsborough, Jean	1940-51	Chuanchow	Medical
Dr N Tunnell, Phyllis	1940-51	Chuanchow	Medical
Revd B Anderson, Clare	1946-48	Chuanchow	Pastoral
Revd H D Beeby, Joyce	1946-49	Amoy	Pastoral
Dr D Short, Jean	1948-50	Chuanchow	Medical
Miss M Fraser	1926-50	Changpu, Amoy	Pastoral, teaching
Miss D Pearce	1933-50	Amoy	Kindergarten training
Mrs W Jett	1934-50	Yungchun	Pastoral
Miss K Duncan	1935-50	Chuanchow	Educational
Miss D Keningale	1940-49	Chuanchow	Nursing
Miss A Riddoch	1946-48	Yungchun	Evangelistic

Lingtung, Swatow/Hakka

Revd H F Wallace, Hera	1903-47	Swatow	Educational, Theol. educ.
Dr N D Fraser, Peggy	1922-50	Swatow, Swabue	Medical
Dr H R Worth, Betty	1928-48	Swatow	Medical
Revd G F Mobbs, Muriel	1930-50	Wukingfu	Pastoral
Revd J Waddell, Kathleen	1932-50	Swatow, Swabue	Pastoral
Dr S L Strange, Margaret	1937-50	Swatow	Medical
Revd R A Elder, Joan	1941-50	Wukingfu, Shanghang	Pastoral
Revd G A Hood, Beth	1945-50	Swatow, Chao-an	Pastoral, Theol. educ.
Mr J Graf, Clare	1947-51	Swatow	Hospital administration
Revd P Montgomery, Mary	1948-50	Chao-an	Pastoral
Dr P A Shave, Margaret	1949-51	Swatow	Medical
Dr A J Farmer, Audrey	1949-51	Wukingfu	Medical

Miss W J Starkey	1913-50	Wukingfu	Educational, pastoral
Miss M V D Paton	1914-50	Swabue	Educational, pastoral
Miss J M Gilchrist	1916-50	Wukingfu	Pastoral, training
Miss G H J Burt	1921-51	Chao-an	Pastoral, training
Miss F E Starkey	1922-49	Wukingfu	Pastoral
Dr R Milne (Oakley)	1932-51	Swatow	Medical
Miss A L Richards	1932-50	Swatow, Chao-an	Pastoral, teaching
Miss C Downward	1938-50	Swabue	Evangelistic, teaching
Miss E Kenneth	1946-47	Swatow	Nursing

Cheeloo University

| Miss E M Eldrige (Kiesow) | 1948-53 | Cheeloo | Educational |

Formosa/Taiwan

Revd & Mrs W Montgomery	1909-50	Tainan	Pastoral, Theol. educ.
Mr & Mrs L Singleton	1921-57	Tainan	Evangelistic
Revd D & Mrs MacLeod	1928-65	Tainan, Changhua	Pastoral
Revd B Anderson, Clare	1948-65	Tainan	Pastoral, Theol. educ.
Revd H D Beeby, Joyce	1950-72	Tainan	Pastoral, Theol. educ.
Revd J N Whitehorn, Elizabeth	1951-70	Yushan	Theol. educ. Bible Trans.
Dr D Landsborough, Jean	1952-80	Changhua	Medical
Mr W Carruthers, Doreen	1957-66	Tainan	Educational
Mr I N Shepherd, Joan	1958-95	Taichung	Educational
Revd A G D Raynham	1961-67	Tainan	Pastoral
Mr P J Storey, Agnes	1963-80	Yushan, Yuli	Agricultural
Miss G Gauld	1931-65	Tainan	Nursing
Miss M Beattie	1933-49	Tainan	Educational
Miss R MacLeod	1934-55	Tainan	Educational

(from 1955-1971, missionary of the United Church of Canada, but continuing in Tainan)

Miss K E M Moody	1948-85	Tainan	Theol. educ., music
Miss C S Holmes	1950-76	Changhua	Nursing
Miss D Pearce	1951-57	Tainan	Kindergarten training
Miss A Riddoch	1952-75	Tainan, Hsinchu	Evangelistic, Kindergarten training

Miss K Whillas	1957-63	Tainan	Teaching mission staff children
Miss J M Barclay	1957-73	Tainan	Educational
Miss E J Brown	1961-89	Tainan, Taipei	Educational, Admin.
Miss E Crofts (Browne)	1961-70	Changhua	Nursing
Miss L Elliott	1971-76	Changhua	Nursing

Singapore/Malaysia

Revd Anderson A S M	1932-48	Singapore	Pastoral, Chinese/English
Revd T C Gibson, Phyllis	1932-51	Singapore	Pastoral, Chinese/English
Revd R L Richards, Dorothy	1937-47	Singapore, Muar	Pastoral, Chinese/English
Mr & Mrs J Richardson	1937-49	Singapore	Educational
Revd J S Henderson, Daphne	1950-77	Singapore, Muar Kluang, K. Baru	Pastoral, Chinese/English
Mr B Atherton, Margaret	1951-58	Singapore	Educational
Revd R A Elder, Joan	1951-65	Ipoh, J.Bahru,K.Baru	Pastoral, Chinese/English Pastoral,
Revd G A Hood, Beth	1952-72	J.Bahru, Kluang NE Coast Singapore	Pastoral, Chinese/English
Mr R Tully, Kathlyn	1952-63	Singapore	Educational
Revd J R Shad, Mary	1956-60	J.Bahru, Singapore	Pastoral, English
Mr J Swanston, Catherine	1956-64	Kulai	Educational
Revd J Waddell	1956-58	Singapore	Administration
Revd G D Gill, Ruth	1961-64	J.Bahru, Singapore	Pastoral, English
Revd D E Marsden, Mary	1966-74	Singapore	Pastoral, English
Revd R A Irving, Pat	1967-73	K.Baru, Kulai	Pastoral, English
Revd D W Elliott, Odette	1968-72	J.Bahru	Pastoral, English
Miss M M Sirkett	1947-73	Singapore	Educational
Miss A Riddoch	1949-52	Singapore	Educational
Miss C S Holmes	1949-50	Singapore	Nursing
Miss A L Richards	1952-67	Kulai	Pastoral, educational

Pilgrims in Mission *List of Missionaries*

Miss C Downward	1952-72	Singapore, Johore NE Coast	Pastoral, Chinese/English
Miss M Prestige (Honey)	1952-56	Singapore	Educatiomal
Miss G H J Burt	1953-57	Batu Pahat	Pastoral, Chinese/English
Miss L Smith	1954-55	Kulai	Educational
Miss J Dukes (Lovett-Hargis)	1958-62	NE Coast	Pastoral, Chinese/English

Rev J. Waddell also served as an Emergency Administration Officer in Malaya, 1952-56 and with the Leprosy Mission in Hong Kong, 1958-1971

Rajshahi/E Pakistan/Bangladesh

Mr D J Ewart, Edith	1923-49	Rajshahi	Educational
Revd A Macleod, Margaret	1936-55	Rajshahi, Naogaon	Evangelistic/Pastoral
Revd B Dawson, Margaret	1947-61	Naogaon, Rajshahi	Evangelistic/Pastoral
Dr I Patrick, Molly	1948-58	Rajshahi	Medical
Dr A J Farmer, Audrey	1951-55	Rajshahi	Medical
Revd D G Paterson Angelika	1956-59	Rajshahi	Evangelistic/Pastoral
Dr P A Shave, Margaret	1958-59	Rajshahi	Medical
Revd M George, Betty	1959-67	Naogaon	Evangelistic/Pastoral
Revd D Morgan, Elaine	1961-72	Rajshahi, Santals	Evangelistic/Pastoral
Revd R A Irving, Pat	1963-66	Rajshahi	Evangelistic/Pastoral
Miss M Miller	1919-50	Rajshahi	Evang/Training
Miss P Vacher	1921-58	Rajshahi	Educational
Miss E Weaver (Cutts)	1947-50	Rajshahi	Nursing
Miss J Nichols	1948-52	Rajshahi	Evang/Training
Miss J Hope (Paton)	1950-65	Rajshahi	Nursing
Miss B Brittain (Rowe)	1951-54	Rajshahi	Educational
Dr E Connan	1953-74	Rajshahi	Medical
Miss A Bade	1954-57	Rajshahi	Nursing
Miss J Saunders	1958-66 1972-74	Rajshahi	Nursing
Miss M Harlow	1961-62	Rajshahi	Nursing

Miss S Askeland   1966-67   Rajshahi   Nursing
Miss P G Boulton   1969-71   Rajshahi   Educational
Miss J Degenhardt   1970-79   Rajshahi   Nursing

India, Vellore Hospital

Dr & Mrs G D Van Rossum 1965-67   Vellore   Biochemist
Miss J N D Bald   1968-83   Vellore   Occ. Therapist

Amoy Mission Council, 1940

Rev. W. Short, Mrs H.J.P. Anderson, Dr Florence Read, Miss Kathleen Duncan,
Dr David Landsborough, Miss Doris Arrowsmith, Mr Peter Anderson,
Miss Nora Arrowsmith, Rev. Ian Latto, Miss Dorothy Keningale, Mr H.J.P. Anderson,
Dr Norman Tunnell, Mr Robert Tully, Mr R.A. Rogers, Mrs Jett, Mrs Peter Anderson,
Rev. A.S.M. Anderson, Peter John Anderson.

THE LATEST TEN
RECRUITS

Miss Alvinza Riddoch, (1)
Rev. Boris and Mrs. Anderson, (2, 3)
Rev. Robert and Mrs. Elder (4, 5)
Rev. George and Mrs. Hood, (6, 7)
Miss Edna Kenneth, (8)
Rev. Dan and Mrs. Beeby, (9, 10)

The Latest Ten Recruits, 1947

Swatow Mission Hospital Medical Staff,
including Tony Strange, Ruth Milne and Peter Shave, 1950

Interior of Pue-li Theological College Chapel, 1949

Welcomes and Farewells, Chuanchow Hospital, 1940

Lingdong Church Officials in 1949,
left to right, Kui Chi Ien, Toh En Hun, Sheffield Cheng, Lim Tsu Sun

Taiwan Mission Council, English Committee, 1966

Back row: Alastair Raynham, Ivor Shepherd, US colleague, Dan Beeby, Jean Landsborough, David Landsborough, Margaret Barclay, US colleague, Joyce Beeby. *Middle row*: Peter Storey, Elspeth Crofts, Ruth Macleod, Walter Carruthers, US colleague. *Front row*: Joan Shepherd, Doreen Carruthers, Kathleen Moody, Elizabeth Brown, Agnes Storey, US colleague, Elizabeth Whitehorn, John Whitehorn, Christina Holmes, Alvinza Riddoch

v

Ng Bu-tong and Shoki Coe

C.M. Kao and Ruth Kao

Yu Shan Theological College,
Main Building

Tainan Theological College, Early Building

Tunghai University Chapel, Chapel of Light

Changhua Hospital 1965

Hsinchu, Kindergarten
Teacher Training

One of the Early
Mountain Churches

Chang Jung Senior High School, Tainan,
Chaplain's Office

Malaya Mission Council, 1952, EP Missionaries underlined.
Standing: Frank Balchin, Celia Downward, Bernarr Atherton, George Hood, Tom Blakely, Robert Tully, Bob Elder, Agnes Richards.
Seated, second row: Monica Sirkett, Joan Elder, Margaret Atherton, Ivy Balchin, Hester Stewart, Anne Stening, Pearl Fleming, Irene Smith.
Seated, front row: John Fleming, Robert Greer, Beth Hood, John Henderson, Joyce Lovell, Jean Johnston, Babs Neave, Harry Johnston.

Opening Ceremony Procession at the first Christian Church in Trengganu State, 1962

Outdoor Film Evangelism in Johore

A "New Village" Church, Mersing, Johore

Outside the Hendersons' home in Muar, Johore.
Left to right: Agnes Richards, Joyce Lovell, Boris Anderson (visiting OM Secretary), Daphne Henderson, John Henderson with Anita, George Hood.

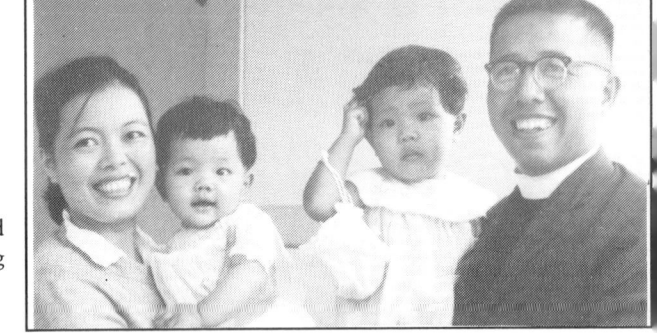

Chen Fu-sheng, Su-Chun and their children, Kluang

Interior of Bethel Church,
Singapore

Noah Chen,
Synod Secretary

Katong Boys' Brigade

Prinsep Street Church,
Singapore

Monica Sirkett and School Prefects, 1954

Church Workers Conference in Penang, 1963

Kluang Church, Ordination of Stephen Tan, 1967

Rajshahi Mission Council and Visiting Deputation, Peggy Moody and Andrew Jamieson, 1951
Back row: Bryan Dawson, Alan Macleod. *Middle row*: Ian Patrick, Molly Patrick, Joan Hope, Peggy Moody, Phyllis Vacher.
Front row: Andrew Jamieson, Margaret Dawson, Margaret Macleod, Joyce Nichol.

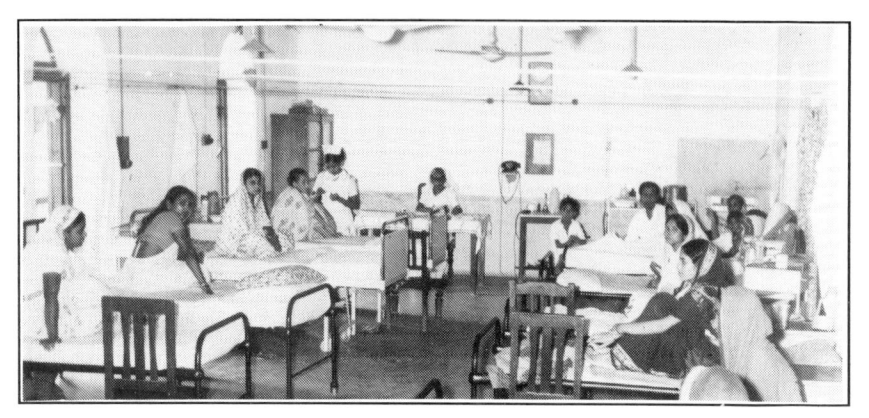

Rajshahi Christian Hospital,
Women's Ward

Treating Cholera in Refugee Camp

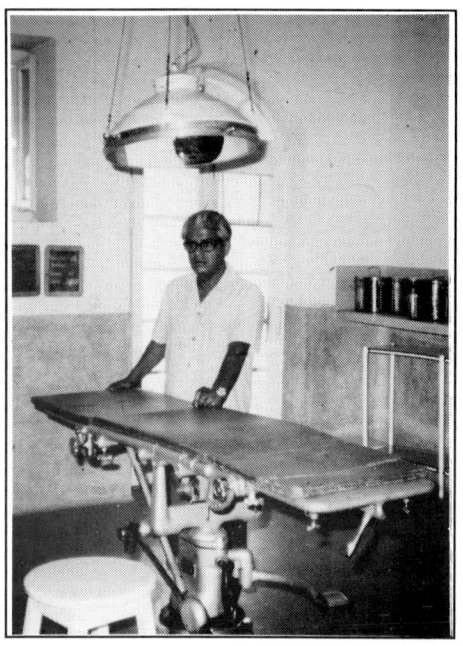

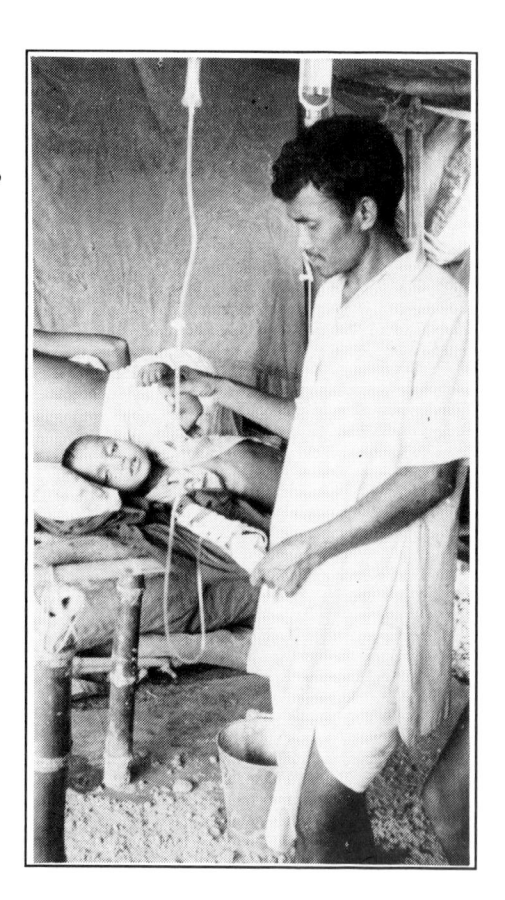

Hospital Superintendent, Dr Malakar
in Operating Theatre

Mission House, Naogaon

Priya Barui

Jean Degenhardt, surrounded

Rajshahi Missionaries, 1966.
Standing: Elizabeth Connan, Joan Hope, Joyce Saunders.
Seated: David Morgan, Elaine Morgan with Gareth,
Pat Irving, Bob Irving

Bolunpur Girls' High School, Rajshahi, Morning Assembly

A Santal Village Church